Flowering
Trees and Shrubs

Flowering
Trees and Shrubs

Richard Bird

Quantum
Books

A QUANTUM BOOK

This book is produced by
Quantum Publishing Ltd.
6 Blundell Street
London N7 9BH

ISBN 1-86160-494-7

QUMFTS

Printed in Singapore by
Star Standard Industries Pte Ltd.

CONTENTS

FOREWORD   *7*

HOW TO USE THE DIRECTORY   8

DIRECTORY OF TREES AND SHRUBS   10

GETTING THE BEST FROM YOUR TREES AND SHRUBS   144

GLOSSARY   155

FOREWORD

by Alan Titchmarsh

Don't ever believe that gardeners are level-headed human beings with infinite patience and a love of all that grows. They are not. They are creatures riddled with prejudice and passions. Just as a love of music does not imply equal appreciation of Mahler and Madonna, Mantovani and Menuhin, so the gardener who loves magnolias may well hate myrtle. But what he will admit is that flowering trees and shrubs are two of the most vital features of his garden, whether it comprises rolling acres or staccato square yards.

There was a time (and it's fortunately passing), when a bedful of dwarf conifers was the height of fashion. Their longevity and continuous season of interest was seen as a brilliant way of making an area "smart" all the year round. Now this is all very well if the "smart" bed is only a part of the garden, but all too often it took over the entire plot, and what could have been a garden of blossoms and blooms, foliage and fun, turned into something redolent of a cemetery.

Gardening must retain one of its greatest assets – that of changing seasons. If the seasons cannot be seen to change because everything is evergreen, then boredom sets in. Transience is important. Who wants roses in the middle of winter? Not me. Who wants chrysanthemums in spring? Not me. Anticipation is a pleasure. The travelling hopefully towards the season of a certain flower makes the arrival all the more enjoyable.

In short, flowering trees and shrubs make the garden exciting. Some of them are generous, not only with the quantity of bloom, but also with the length of the flowering season. Others are profligate for a fortnight and naked thereafter. There must be room for both. The rashness of lilac – cramming all its heavy heads into three weeks in June – the bravery of witch hazel – squirting out fragrant yellow spiders in midwinter – and the sheer mind-blowing generosity of the flowering cherry provide thrills that no conifer ever aspired to.

Maybe I'm a romantic, but romance is as important in gardening as is the saving of labour, the suppression of weeds and the screening from neighbours, all of which trees and shrubs can provide as a sideline.

Richard Bird has picked out the very best. Plants that will display for you the variety of forms and shapes and colours that are seemingly inexhaustible, and also the scents that tease in sun and snow.

You won't like *all* the plants he describes, but some of them will cause you to embark upon an eventful love affair. It's a well-known fact that there's no cure for this sickness, and as any sage who knows his onions will tell you, it gets worse with age. But these mistresses are not fickle jades. Yes; some of them are temperamental, and some of them will take a deal of pleasing. But once you've sorted out their likes and dislikes they'll give you ample recompense for your trouble. Turn the pages and get involved. Richard Bird gives you all the encouragement to become hooked for life.

HOW TO USE THE DIRECTORY

There are many ways in which one could organize a list of plants. The simplest – and the method we have chosen – is in alphabetical order, but plants can also be arranged according to type (shrub, climber and so on), flowering period, by whether they prefer sun or shade, or by whether they are deciduous or evergreen. All of these properties may govern the selection of plants for a garden, and for this reason each main entry in the book includes a box containing symbols. These summarize the chief properties of the plant and a zone number indicates the hardiness of the plants in that entry.

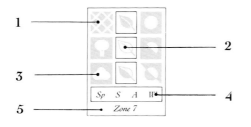

Symbols

1 This column indicates, reading from the top down, whether the plant is a climber, a tree or a shrub. Climbers are defined as plants that need support of some kind, whether it be a wall, a trellis or another plant. Some climbers support themselves by means of roots or tendrils; others must be tied to wires or some form of framework.

The difference between trees and shrubs becomes blurred where the two meet. As a general rule, however, trees are single-stemmed and tall, while shrubs are shorter and are normally bushy in appearance. Where a genus comprises trees and shrubs, both symbols are given.

2 The middle column refers to leaves – from top to bottom, evergreen, deciduous and semi-evergreen. The evergreen symbol indicates those plants that retain their leaves during the winter. Like all plants, these shed their leaves, but this happens throughout the year, a few at a time, so that it is hardly noticeable. Deciduous plants drop all their leaves during the autumn and remain bare throughout the winter. Again, there is a grey area between the two: semi-evergreen plants generally hold some or all of their leaves, but a severe winter could cause them all to be dropped.

3 The right-hand column indicates the light conditions preferred by the plant. Many plants will only grow well in either sun or shade, but there are others that will grow equally well in either. Symbols are given for all three categories. Many of the plants that are listed as liking sun will tolerate a little light shade, but they will not flower or perform as well in shady conditions. Shade should generally be considered to be light or dappled: very few plants will grow in full shade, but where this is the case, the fact will be noted in the text.

4 This panel gives an indication of the flowering period – spring, summer, autumn or winter. This is difficult to give with any greater degree of accuracy, as it will vary according to the timing and length of the seasons, which in turn vary from one zone to another. Some plants are prone to occasional repeat flowering, prolonging the season well after the main flush of flowers is past.

Plant hardiness

One of the big questions facing a gardener when choosing a plant is whether it will prove hardy in that particular area. Hardiness is a strange phenomenon: a plant may thrive in one garden and die in another only a short distance away. Certainly, there are plants in my garden that would not survive in the valley below, which is only 30 metres or so lower. This valley is a notorious frost hollow and, although situated in a mild, temperate zone, has recorded frosts in every month of the year.

Hardiness is not only affected by the cold: winter wet plays a large part in plant losses. Many plants, for example *Cistus*, will survive much colder temperatures in a free-draining soil. Very few trees and shrubs like a soil that is permanently wet, and every effort should be made to improve the drainage.

Having mentioned the difficulty of defining whether a plant can be expected to be hardy within the confines of a limited area, the reader will appreciate the difficulty of predicting hardiness on a national or international scale, where the variation in climate is enormous. I have tried to overcome this problem in two ways.

Firstly, the plant descriptions state the minimum temperature at which a plant is known to survive, though in many cases individual plants may survive at far colder temperatures if local conditions are otherwise favourable. Certainly, if plants are given protection against frost and winds they should be able to survive temperatures below the minimum stated in the text. The protection may take the form of the shelter of other plants or, better still, a warm wall, or it may be hessian sacking or bracken. Surprisingly, snow also gives good protection, although it can cause physical damage to some species, by weighing down branches and breaking them.

Secondly, a hardiness zone number is given at the bottom of the box next to each genus (5). This scale was originally devised in the US, but has increasingly been used, in other areas throughout the world. The zones are graded according to the lowest range of temperatures at which a plant will normally survive. Thus a plant listed under

Zone chart

ZONE	CENTIGRADE	FAHRENHEIT
1	below $-46°$	below $-50°$
2	$-46°$ to $-40°$	$-50°$ to $-40°$
3	$-40°$ to $-34°$	$-40°$ to $-30°$
4	$-34°$ to $-28°$	$-30°$ to $-20°$
5	$-28°$ to $-22°$	$-20°$ to $-10°$
6	$-22°$ to $-16°$	$-10°$ to $0°$
7	$-16°$ to $-12°$	$0°$ to $10°$
8	$-12°$ to $-6°$	$10°$ to $20°$
9	$-6°$ to $-1°$	$20°$ to $30°$
10	$-1°$ to $4°$	$30°$ to $40°$

zone 7 will survive temperatures down to between $-16°C$ and $-12°C$ ($0°F$ and $10°F$).

Unfortunately, trees and shrubs, unlike herbaceous plants, are generally expensive, and while it can be exciting to gamble with a plant of borderline hardiness, this can be costly. Fortunately, there is a host of beautiful trees and shrubs that will survive at very low temperatures, and there will always be a wide range from which to choose if you prefer to play safe.

Abelia

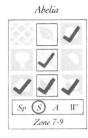

Abelia

ABELIA

THIS IS AN ATTRACTIVE small group of deciduous and semi-evergreen plants from eastern Asia and Mexico. They are characterized by their bunches of trumpet-like flowers, which come in a range of pink and white through to reddish purple, with persistent red sepals, which remain after the flower has dropped. Most species flower from early to midsummer, while *A. × grandiflora* flowers into the autumn. All species have a long flowering period. They are not very quick growing, but most species will eventually make a shrub of 1.5-2m (5-6ft).

They thrive in any fertile soil as long as it is free draining. Full sun is preferred for best flowering, but light shade is tolerated. Some species are on the tender side and should be given the protection of a wall, and none are very tolerant of salty wind.

Abelias are beautiful bushes and their long flowering period makes them an ideal choice for a prime site, perhaps at the back of a summer/autumn border. They are suitable for shrubberies or mixed herbaceous borders; they make fine specimen plants. They associate particularly well with other pink-flowered plants as well as those with magenta and purple flowers. Abelia can be used as an

Abeliophyllum

Abeliophyllum

Abelia × grandiflora 'COPPER GLOW'

informal hedge, but the plants will not flower freely if continually clipped.

Propagation is from semi-ripe – first year mature – cuttings in late summer. Pruning should be restricted to removal of a few of the older stems from the base and any dead wood. Flowers appear on two- or three-year-old wood, so any regular pruning will reduce the amount of flowers.

A. floribunda has bright red-purple flowers that appear at the beginning of the summer and mid- to deep green leaves with a glossy sheen. It is not a very hardy plant (−5°C; 23°F) and needs the protection of a wall.

Abelia × grandiflora is sometimes called 'GLOSSY ABELIA' because of its shiny leaves. It is one of the best of the abelias, with large pink and white, slightly fragrant tubular flowers appearing over a long period from midsummer until autumn. It is semi-evergreen and although some leaves drop in the autumn a large proportion are retained throughout the winter unless the weather is harsh. The leaves are a glossy green with a purplish-bronze tinge. *A. grandiflora* is quite hardy and will take temperatures down to −12°C (10°F). There is a good variegated-leaved form called 'FRANCIS MASON'.

A. schumannii is a smaller, deciduous shrub that has large flowers – lilac pink, shading to white – and is another plant that is on the tender side (−5°C; 23°F), flowering from the early summer. There is a hardier hybrid with *A. × grandiflora* called 'EDWARD GOUCHER', which was raised in the early part of this century. The flowers are more purple than those of *A. schumannii* .

Abeliophyllum

WHITE FORSYTHIA

A GENUS WITH ONLY one species, namely *A. distichum*, this is an untidy shrub that would have little merit if it did not flower in the winter or early spring when there is not much else about. It is very similar to *Forsythia*, to which it is related, both in habit and shape of flower.

Abeliophyllum distichum

The flowers are white tinged with pink, appearing before the leaves, and they have the advantage of being fragrant.

Abeliophyllum does not take long to reach its mature height of 2m (6ft) or higher, if against a wall. It is not fussy about soil and is hardy to about −20°C (−4°F).

This shrub is magnificent for the short time it is in flower, with branches clothed in fragrant white flowers, but for the rest of the year it is a bit of a liability. It favours a wall position and prefers sun. The flower association is unimportant as there is little else out at

the time of flowering, so it is best fitted in between other shrubs and plants, where it will not be noticed throughout the rest of the year. The ideal position would be at the back of an herbaceous border, where it would receive sun but would be concealed by the summer growth of more attractive plants.

Abeliophyllum can be propagated from semi-ripe cuttings taken in late summer. Pruning should be restricted to removing some of the old growth after flowering as the flowers come on the old wood.

Abutilon

ABUTILON

THIS IS A LARGE genus of over 100 species, most of which are tender. Most species are evergreens, with thin stems and maple-shaped leaves. The flowers are bright, often with a pendulous bell shape in various colours. Abutilons grow quite quickly to their mature size of about 2m (6ft) or more.

All species prefer a rich, moisture retentive soil in a sunny position. None are perfectly hardy (−5°C; 23°F) and those that will grow outside prefer to grow against a wall. They make ideal plants for growing in a cool conservatory, either in pots or a raised bed, where they will flower intermittently for most of the year. Conservatory plants can be moved out into the garden during the summer.

Some varieties are hardy enough to plant out as free-standing plants. These, as well as plants raised in a greenhouse and moved outside for the summer, can be planted in any sunny position. The large green leaves and the range of colours in the flowers make them versatile in their positioning. In colder areas and with the more tender species, plant against a wall. The thin pliant stems make it easy to train the branches to get maximum advantage in the display of the flowers.

Propagation is from semi-ripe cuttings in summer. A third of the old wood and any dead material should be pruned out in spring.

Abutilon megapotamicum is one of the

Abutilon × *suntense*

Abutilon

Sp (*S*) *A* *W*
Zone 9

Abutilon megapotamicum

form, 'ALBUM'. 'VERONICA TENNANT' is a good form with large pale mauve flowers. The leaves are large and shaped like grape leaves, as its name *vitifolium* ("vine leaved") implies. Like the others, this species will prove tender in the colder districts and protection from a wall is a help. As well as from cuttings, this species comes readily from seed and will often self-sow around the parent plant.

There is also a large number of named hybrids available from the bigger nurseries. A. 'ASHFORD RED', which has pinkish red flowers, is one of the commonest. Another popular hybrid is A. 'KENTISH BELLE', with orange flowers. A. 'CANARY BIRD' and A. 'GOLDEN FLEECE' have yellow flowers and A. 'BOULE DE NEIGE' has white.

Acacia

Zone 9 — Sp S A W

hardiest species. It has curious yellow funnel-shaped flowers emerging from an inflated red calyx. From the centre of the flower comes a column of dark purple stamens. They are solitary and spring from the leaf axils. The leaves are not as large as other species and are more ovate, with toothing round the margins. The whole is a rather loose, graceful shrub. There is a very attractive variegated variety, 'VARIEGATUM', that has strong yellow mottling on the leaves.

A. × *milleri* is of garden origin and is a more tender version of A. *megapotamicum*, with larger leaves and orange petals with red veins and crimson stamens. This is better treated as a conservatory plant.

A. × *suntense* is a vigorous hybrid between A. *ochensii* and A. *vitifolium*. It has large violet-blue or purple cup-shaped flowers. Relatively tender, it needs protection or constant renewal.

A. *vitifolium* has a more tree-like shape and can reach 3m (10ft) or more in favourable positions. The flowers are a flatter shape than some of the other species. They are often borne several at a time in small bunches. They vary from a pale to deep mauve and there is a white

Acacia

ACACIA, MIMOSA, WATTLE

THIS IS A VERY LARGE GENUS of some 800 species of shrubs and trees, mostly Australian. They have very distinctive foliage and flowers, both of which are very well known from their appearances in florists' shops. Acacias have very divided, bipinnate foliage, silver or grey in colour, and clouds of fluffy yellow flowers.

Acacia armata

Although the flowers belong to the pea family (Leguminosae) they are most unpea-like as they have minute petals and a mass of fine stamens that makes up the individual flowers.

They are all somewhat tender, −5°C (23°F) being the lowest temperature at which they will survive, but they are so attractive that they are worth growing in colder districts even if they only last a few years before they succumb to a particularly cold season. If they do survive, and many will, they grow quite quickly and soon reach a height of 6 or 7m (20ft) and up to 10m (33ft) as trees.

Acacias will grow in most garden soils that are not too alkaline. Because they are tender, the aspect is important; they should be protected from the cold winds, preferably against a south-facing wall. They also make excellent conservatory subjects provided they are replaced before they get too large.

An acacia has an all-the-year-round appeal, which means that it certainly has a place as a specimen tree. The problem of siting in many areas, as already mentioned, is really to do with climatic conditions in the garden rather than with plant association. It looks good against a blue sky, but while it is still low enough to be of shrub-like proportions it is well set off by other green-foliaged shrubs and trees.

Propagation takes place either from seed or from semi-ripe cuttings in early summer. Pruning, other than the removal of any dead or damaged branches, is not required.

Acacia armata, known as Kangaroo Thorn, is an evergreen shrub reaching about 3m (10ft) high. It has small finely cut leaves and thorny spines on the stems. The attraction is the masses of bright yellow flowers in spring. It is best grown in colder areas as a conservatory or greenhouse plant.

A. baileyana, the Cootamundra Wattle, is one of the finest of the acacias, with a graceful habit, foliage with a grey, waxy sheen and racemes of small powder-puffs of bright yellow flowers. Just as with *A. armata*, this is often seen growing as a large shrub.

The commonest and hardiest of the trees is *A. dealbata*, the Silver Wattle. As its common name suggests, it has silver foliage. This is very finely cut, almost like a fern, and the tree is covered with clouds of fragrant, fluffy, yellow flowers in spring, or even winter if grown in a conservatory. This is the species that florists use as the cut flower "mimosa".

A. longifolia, Sydney Golden Wattle, is a shrub with long narrow leaves and bright yellow flowers. It can survive outside as long as it has protection from a warm wall.

A. melanoxylon, Blackwood Acacia, is also fairly hardy and in its native habitat can reach over 30m (100ft) in height, though it is unlikely to do so in cooler climates. As well as the adult lance-shaped leaves it also produces a more "mimosa"-like foliage when young. Again it has yellow flowers in spring.

Many more species are available. None will take temperatures much below freezing, but they are worth experimenting with in mild areas.

Acacia baileyana

Aesculus

HORSE CHESTNUT, BUCKEYE

A FAMILIAR AND WELL-LOVED TREE, this has large leaves, composed of between five and seven large leaflets, and huge conical panicles

Aesculus

Zone 5

Aesculus hippocastanum

of white flowers. These are followed in autumn by the bright, shining brown "conkers" that few school children can resist. There are a number of equally good species that are not difficult to find. These vary in stature, leaf shape and flower colour, the main alternative to white being pink or red. They are all very hardy, taking temperatures down to −25°C (−13°F) or even below. The majority make substantial trees of up to 25m (80ft).

Horse chestnuts will grow in a wide range of soils as long as they are not waterlogged. The larger limbs can become brittle in time, so protection from wind is helpful but not essential. They will take light shade but look best in full sun, where they flower freely.

These statuesque trees are really more suited to a parkland setting than a garden, unless it is a large one. There are, however, some species that are well suited to the garden. These look extremely good as specimen trees on a large expanse of grass and they look equally striking when they rise, covered with candles of blossom, from among other trees, particularly if they are backed by the green foliage of taller trees around them.

Propagation is readily achieved from seed. Pruning is rarely needed except for the occasional removal of dead branches.

Aesculus × *carnea* is frequently seen in parks and avenues. It is characterized by its pinky-red flowers and by the fruit case being smooth instead of spiky. This is a smaller tree than the common form, *A. hippocastanum*, but can still reach 12m (40ft). This, plus the advantage of being slower growing, means that it can be considered for medium-sized gardens. It is a cross between *A. hippocastanum* and *A. pavia*. The best form is 'BRIOTTI', which has deep red flowers. 'PLANTIERENSIS' has pink flowers and is finding favour in many parks as it is sterile, thus avoiding the danger of damage caused by little boys seeking conkers.

A. hippocastanum, with its masses of large candles of white flowers with a red blotch at the base of the petals, is the true horse chestnut. Best seen at a distance, it needs a lot of space. Children can plant a horse chestnut as a conker and then watch it grow during their lifetime, as it grows quite quickly, but this speed ensures that it will soon outgrow a small garden. Its roots are thirsty and hungry, which makes it unsuitable to grow near buildings or where it is intended to have borders of any kind. The form 'BAUMANNII' (also known as 'FLORE PLENO') has double flowers and is sterile.

A. indica, Indian Chestnut, is another large tree, this time with white flowers flushed with a tinge of pink and yellow. Its leaves are shiny and slightly folded, and it gives good autumn colour. The form 'SYDNEY PEARCE' has very large flowers and darker leaves.

Aesculus × *carnea*

Amelanchier canadensis

A. *parviflora* is a true shrub, reaching only 3-4m (10-13ft). The white flower spikes are large but not as solid as those of the common forms. It has the advantage of flowering later in the season, and offers good autumn colour.

A. *pavia*, Red Buckeye, is one of the smaller species forming only a small tree or shrub of 4m (13ft), making it suitable for the smaller garden. Its "candles" are not so large as those of other species, but they are a good shade of bright red. 'ATROSANGUINEUS' has deeper red flowers than the type-plant and 'HUMILIS' is low growing, more shrub-like.

Amelanchier

SNOWY MESPILUS, JUNE BERRY

THIS IS A GENUS of deciduous shrubs and small trees from North America that have good flowers, fine autumn colouring and edible fruit. They are as good all-rounders as they sound. The flowers are pure white and hang in loose racemes in great profusion during the spring, often before the leaves appear. They are not all that long-lasting. The edible round, black berries follow the flowering in the summer. The leaves are a light green, turning

to good fiery colours in autumn. Hardiness should not be a problem as amelanchiers will survive to −25°C (−13°F) or more. Moderate in stature, they will eventually reach 5m (16ft) on maturity, but they are slow growing and will take a long time to reach this height. They tend to produce suckers, forming a bush as wide as it is high.

Amelanchiers are tolerant of a wide range of soils, but prefer the ground to be moisture retentive rather than waterlogged. They are hardy, so there is no problem in siting. Sun is preferred but they will tolerate some shade.

Being a good, versatile shrub, an amelanchier can be given a prominent position, either isolated as a specimen or in a key position in a shrubbery or mixed border. If the berries are to be eaten, it should be accessible.

Amelanchiers can be propagated from the abundantly produced seed – each fruit contains several – or by layering the pliable branches. Since amelanchiers produce suckers, these can be separated from the parent plant during the winter to become new bushes. No pruning is required apart from a general tidying up of the plant.

Amelanchier canadensis is a tall, erect bush that produces a lot of suckers. It has upright racemes of pure white flowers and, later, black fruit. The leaves are downy when young but

Amelanchier

Sp S A W
Zone 5

Amelanchier lamarckii

this disappears as the season progresses. *A. canadensis* has been used in gardens as a blanket name covering several other species, including *A. laevis* and *A. lamarckii.*

A. laevis can be either a small tree or a large bush. The leaves have emerged by flowering time.

A. lamarckii is one of the most popular species because of its beauty at flowering time. The flowers appear before the leaves and are white, sometimes with a pink tinge. The leaves are a coppery pink when they first emerge, turning green and finally a good orange-red in the autumn. The fruit is purple-black. There are two forms of note: 'BALLERINA', which has large white flowers, and 'RUBESCENS' in which the flowers are tinged with pink.

Andromeda

Andromeda

BOG ROSEMARY

THIS IS A VERY small genus, but a delightful one for all its lack of numbers. There is in practice only one species in cultivation, *A. polifolia.* This is a low-growing, evergreen shrub not reaching much above 50cm (20in). The flowers, available in varying shades of pink, are shaped like urns, and hang from the tips of the reddish-brown stems from late spring

Andromeda polifolia

onwards. The leaves are quite short (2.5cm; 1in) and narrow. Bog rosemary is fairly hardy, taking temperatures down to −10°C (14°F).

It is a member of the ericaceous family, which means that it is a lime hater. Acid, peaty soils are its preference, although it will grow in more neutral soils. This is a plant that does not appreciate very hot weather, so the soil should be kept moist and cool. The best situation to achieve this is light shade, but bog rosemary will take full sun if there is sufficient moisture for the roots.

This plant makes an ideal carpeting shrub for a shady area as it gently spreads by the aid of underground runners. It can be used in the rock garden, particularly in its compact forms, and snowdrops can be planted under it so that they poke their heads up through the foliage in the late winter, but have died down by the time the bog rosemary comes into flower.

Propagation can take place from late-summer, softwood cuttings. No pruning is necessary except to keep the plant tidy.

There are numerous forms available, the differences lying mainly in the shade of pink of the flowers or their size. There are also some particularly fine white forms, such as *A.p.* 'ALBA' or the beautiful compact form introduced by Roy Elliott, *A.p.* 'COMPACTA ALBA'. There are quite a number of other compact forms that are very useful for the rock garden, the commonest of these being *A.p.* 'COMPACTA' and the smallest *A.p.* 'MINIMA' with 'NANA' in between the two.

Another plant that is occasionally seen is *A. glaucophylla.* It is debatable whether this is a species in its own right or just a form of *A. polifolia* – either way it does not really matter. This flowers later than the main species; the flower stalks are shorter and the undersides of its leaves are quite hairy.

Aralia

Aralia

ANGELICA TREE

ONLY A FEW OF this small genus of trees and shrubs are in cultivation. Besides their fine

Aralia elata 'AUREOVARIEGATA'

The most commonly available species is *Aralia elata*. This has two variegated forms: 'AUREOVARIEGATA' has margins and blotches of golden yellow, and 'VARIEGATA' sports creamy white markings. The type-plant can sucker rapidly in warmer climates, but the variegated forms should be better behaved in these conditions.

Arbutus

STRAWBERRY TREE

Arbutus

Zone 8

KNOWN AS THE STRAWBERRY TREE because its orange-red fruit resembles strawberries, this plant has the happy habit of fruiting at the same time as it is flowering. The round red berries are well set-off against the white bells of the flowers, which resemble lily-of-the-valley. The foliage is evergreen, with leathery, ovate leaves. Arbutus will eventually form trees but they are extremely slow growing and so are often considered as shrubs. They are quite hardy, taking temperatures to −10°C (14°F); hard frosts may cut a shrub back, but it will usually regenerate.

Although it is a member of the Ericaceae, the strawberry tree will tolerate limy conditions, though it will thrive best in a more acid soil. It has a preference for light shade but will take full sun.

Arbutus unedo

foliage, they are particularly useful for their late-autumn flowering. The flowering is quite spectacular, with small white flowers clothing panicles, 30-60cm (1-2ft) long, that almost cover the top of the plant. The leaves are also very long, sometimes up to 1.2m (4ft). These vast leaves are bipinnate, so that each leaf appears to be composed of numerous smaller leaves. A further curiosity about the leaves is that they tend to grow at the end of stems, appearing rather like ruffs. The trees do not grow too tall for the average garden, reaching only 4m (13ft) on maturity, but they produce spiky suckers that can harbour weeds and will soon turn the tree into a shrub unless they are removed. Aralia are hardy, surviving temperatures down to −15°C (5°F) or below.

They will accept most soils, but prefer ground that is not too dry. Although aralia are hardy they prefer a sunny position, and a site protected from strong wind is a good idea, to prevent damage to the foliage.

These plants make a bold statement and should be sited as a feature in a mixed border or in a prominent position away from the wind. They are lost when grown among other shrubs, unless planted in the foreground. The variegated forms look particularly good against a darker background.

Propagation is achieved by removing some of the suckers. No pruning is required.

This is a splendid specimen shrub or tree and stands well by itself. Some species have very fine peeling red bark that looks particularly well in winter or evening light, in which case a position should be found that makes the most of this feature.

Propagation is usually from seed except where particular varieties are wanted. These are grafted onto seedlings of *A. unedo*. They do not transplant very well, so seedlings should be container-grown and planted into their final position as soon as possible. No pruning is required, except to remove any dead wood. If necessary the shrub can be cut back hard or even used for indoor foliage decoration, but bear in mind the slowness of growth.

Arbutus andrachne has peeling cinnamon-red bark on its older branches. This species flowers in the spring and produces orange-red, smooth-skinned fruit.

A. × *andrachnoides* is a hybrid between *A. andrachne* and *A. unedo*, but with even more richly-coloured bark than its parents. The flowers are produced in late autumn or winter.

A. menziesii, Madrona, has a smooth bark that peels to reveal the terracotta colour of the new bark. The flowers appear in the spring. This is a little more tender than the other species.

A. unedo is the commonest of the arbutuses. Splendid, mature specimens can be seen in Ireland, which is one of its native habitats, particularly in Killarney (it is sometimes known as the Killarney Strawberry Tree). It has fibrous, rich brown bark. Masses of white flowers, tinged with pink, are produced at the tips of the stems in autumn at the same time as the rough-surfaced, red fruit.

Arctostaphylos uva-ursi

including Britain and America. It belongs to the heather family and has typical ericaceous, pink, bell-shaped flowers in spring to be followed by red, globular fruit. The leaves are small and glossy.

Bearberry is hardy down to at least −15°C (5°F). The mature height should not present a problem even in miniature gardens, as it seldom exceeds a few inches.

Bearberries must have an acid, lime-free soil, and ideally a position that gets full sun and allows the plants to run at will, though they will tolerate light shade.

They make attractive, evergreen ground cover and are eminently suitable for interplanting between small shrubs that are expected to grow larger eventually and fill the gaps, particularly other ericaceous plants such as rhododendrons. In addition, bearberries can be underplanted with small bulbs that disappear back below the creeping stems after flowering. Being salt tolerant they are suitable for seaside gardens.

Propagation is easily undertaken from cuttings. No pruning is necessary except to tidy the shrub.

There are two forms of *Arctostaphylos uva-ursi* for which it is worth looking. *A.u.* 'NANA' is a compact version of the type and has the advantage that it does not run, so that it can be used safely on the rock garden. *A. nevadensis* is usually given specific status but is generally assumed to be either a form of *A. uva-ursi* or a very close ally. It is very similar to the latter in appearance.

Arctostaphylos

Sp S A W

Zone 7

Arctostaphylos

BEARBERRY

THESE LOW-GROWING SHRUBS are excellent plants and make very useful ground cover. The species that is commonly in cultivation is *A. uva-ursi*, which is native to most of the cooler temperate areas of the northern hemisphere,

Banksia

BANKSIA

THIS IS A GENUS of trees and shrubs native to Australia. The flowers are in upright cylindrical spikes. Their colour variations are based mainly on yellows and reds. The evergreen leaves vary considerably in shape but are usually quite leathery with fine down on the underside. Banksia vary in height from relatively small shrubs of 2m (6ft) or so, up to full-grown trees of 12m (40ft). They are unfortunately tender and will not tolerate more than a very mild frost. They can be grown in greenhouses or conservatories in colder areas, though they require cool nights if they are to achieve maximum growth and bloom. Most are salt tolerant and can be grown beside the sea.

Banksias need a lime-free soil, but are quite happy in relatively poor soils. They are susceptible to drought so need adequate water, but they should not be over-watered, especially if grown in conservatory or greenhouse. Full sun should be provided.

These are definitely trees and shrubs to be grown as specimen plants; to be admired in their own right. As already indicated, they are particularly worth considering for gardens near the sea.

Propagation is from seed, or, with more

Banksia coccinea

Banksia speciosa

difficulty, from cuttings of ripened wood. No pruning is necessary.

Banksia coccinea, Scarlet Banksia, is a shrub up to 5m (16ft) high, with, as its name implies, scarlet flowers at the ends of its arching branches.

B. ericifolia has large spikes of yellow flowers. The leaves are small and narrow. It can reach up to 4m (13ft) in height.

B. grandis is another yellow-flowered species with spikes that get up to 30cm (1ft) in length. The shrub itself grows up to 12m (40ft) in the wild but much less in cultivation.

B. serrata has red flowers that are rounder than many of the others. The leaves are deeply toothed. This species will grow up to 6m (20ft) and is a good coastal plant.

B. speciosa is a smaller plant, reaching up to 2m (6ft). The flowers are greenish yellow with red stigmas and are held in a dense spike. The pinnate leaves are long and narrow.

Berberis

BARBERRY

THIS IS A VERY large genus of over 500 species in the wild. In the garden we also have a generous range from which to choose, with over 130 species and varieties currently available. The

Banksia

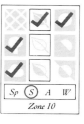

Sp (S) A W
Zone 10

Berberis

(Sp) (S) A W
Zone 7

Berberis darwinii

reason for their popularity is simply that they are good plants: fine clusters of bright flowers, scented in some species; good foliage, some evergreen, others deciduous, with excellent autumn tints, and masses of brightly-coloured red berries. The main objection to them is the thorns that most species bear – small pieces of pruning always seem to find their way into borders and finally into fingers during weeding sessions. But even the thorns have a bonus, as they make berberis a good plant for protective hedges. The hardiness of berberis does not seem to be in doubt; most types will take temperatures down to −15°C (5°F) and many will survive far lower temperatures. There is a good variation in height, from dwarf shrubs of 30cm (1ft) to taller shrubs of 3m (10ft) or so.

The versatility of the plant is continued in its choice of soil and site. It is adaptable, transplanting easily, and it is suitable for virtually any soil and will happily put up with full sun or quite dense shade. However, as with most flowering shrubs, the denser the shade the more straggly the plant is liable to be, and the flowers will be less numerous.

Berberis will fit into a wide range of positions, and can be used in a shrubbery or a mixed border, or grown as a specimen bush. The leaves are small on the whole, but range in colour from bright green to dark purple,

making this a valuable foliage plant to consider when devising a colour scheme. Its rather hot yellow or orange flowers in spring can make positioning critical, but in a mixed border berberis provides this mass of colour early in the season and is only offering foliage colour when the main border comes alive. The purple-leaved varieties look particularly good if sited so that the sun strikes through the foliage or illuminates it in the evening. Because of its tolerance of shade, berberis is valuable in north-facing borders, for example on the north side of a house. Mass plantings of berberis can look very effective, or they can be ranged in a line to form an impenetrable hedge.

Propagation is easy, either from cuttings taken in late summer or from seed. Some species self-sow themselves, giving a constant supply of new plants. The cultivars, however, are not likely to come completely true from seed, so special forms should always be propagated from cuttings. Pruning is not generally required, though bushes will need tidying up, but it is a good idea to remove some of the old wood to encourage new growth. Flowering takes place on old wood, so constant clipping will reduce the amount of flowers produced. Any pruning should take place immediately after flowering.

Berberis aggregata is a deciduous shrub with yellow flowers in early summer. Its toothed leaves colour well in autumn, when it also produces masses of red berries.

B. buxifolia is a widely available form that is partially evergreen. It has single yellow flowers with purple fruit in autumn. This species is best known in the dwarf compact form 'NANA', that slowly grows to an eventual height of about 45cm (1.5ft). 'NANA' is more shy-flowering than the type-plant. Another cultivar is 'AUREO-MARGINATA', in which the leaves are edged in yellow.

B. darwinii is a popular evergreen species with small, toothed, shiny green leaves. In spring it is covered in masses of hanging panicles of golden-yellow flowers and in autumn with blue-black fruit. It suckers freely, forming a dense shrub, which makes it a good plant for a hedge along a north border.

Berberis × stenophylla

B. gagnepainii is one of the larger-leaved forms, with foliage that resembles holly leaves with forward-pointing spines. This evergreen plant produces yellow flowers in spring and black berries later in the year. It suckers and has thorns, both of which make it of good hedging potential.

B. julianae has long narrow leaves and long, somewhat vicious thorns. The yellow flowers are held in tight clusters and have a strong sweet scent. The plant loses some leaves in autumn, the colouring of which, before they fall, can give a touch of contrast to the remainder. It has blue-black fruit.

B. linearifolia is a mass of orange blossom in the spring, contrasted against the narrow green leaves that clothe the shrub all year round. The fruit is black. This is quite a lax, loosely-growing bush, and there is a cultivar, 'ORANGE KING', that has very strong colour.

B. ottawensis is a deciduous species and contains one of the finest of all the berberises. The name *ottawensis* covers a whole series of hybrids raised from crossing *B. thunbergii* and *B. vulgaris*. Among these, 'SUPERBA' lives up to its name and is truly superb, with rich bronzy-red leaves in the summer, turning to a vivid crimson in autumn. The flowers that smother the plant in a mass of dark yellow in spring produce brilliant red berries to add to the autumn colour.

B. × stenophylla is a dense shrub with long arching stems covered in golden yellow flowers in spring. This berberis has a good strong scent and vies with the previous species as being the best of the barberries. Its leaves are very narrow; green on the topside and silvery underneath. The species can be a bit overpowering in all but the larger borders, but it makes a good specimen plant. There are quite a number of excellent cultivars, several of which are smaller in stature and are red in bud, opening to yellow or orange.

B. thunbergii is the third candidate for the title of best of the genus. This has a wide range of cultivars of every hue and size. The best-known one is undoubtedly 'ATROPUR-PUREA', which has yellow flowers touched with red and leaves that are a very good deep red-purple in colour. In autumn this red lightens, yet becomes even more intense, and is accompanied by bright red berries. There is a dwarf version, 'ATROPURPUREA NANA', which is far more compact in habit, reaching only 45-60cm (1½-2ft) in height. 'ROSEGLOW' has the same dark purple leaves but they are spattered with a much paler pink giving a curious but very pleasing effect. 'GOLDRING' is also purple in leaf, but this time the margins take on a golden rim as the season progresses until they finally turn the typical orange-red of autumn. 'AUREA' goes to the other extreme and

Berberis darwinii

has very pale lime-green leaves, that still give a nice orange autumn colour, and there are many more cultivars to look out for.

B. wilsoniae is yet another very good plant. It only reaches about 1.2m (4ft) but it is a spreading plant with quite a wide girth. It comes into its own in the autumn, when its green leaves tint up beautifully to an orange that pleasantly complements the coral-coloured berries that are carried in abundance. The flowers are yellow.

There are many more species and cultivars to explore, in addition to those mentioned here, and a person restricted to only one would be hard put to make a choice. If a garden is small then perhaps several of the more dwarf forms might solve the problem.

Boronia

Sp (S) A W
Zone 10

Boronia

BORONIA

DEPENDING ON THE classification you follow, there are between 50 and 70 species of this compact endemic Australian shrub. Not all are garden-worthy, but quite a number make an attractive addition to the garden. They are all evergreen, with either simple or compound

Boronia heterophylla

pinnate leaves, which in some species are extremely aromatic. The flowers appear in the spring and are star-shaped, with four petals. For the most part, they come in a wide variety of shades of pink. Some are sweetly scented. Boronias vary in height from 50cm to 2m (1½ to 6ft), although one or two species grow higher. Coming from Australia, boronias are best suited to warmer climates and will not tolerate frosts. In colder climates they can be grown in a warm conservatory.

Boronias prefer to be in a free-draining sandy soil that is not overfed. They should not be allowed to become too dry in summer and they do not like too much sun.

They make good compact border plants and can also be grown in tubs. In colder areas, this allows them to be overwintered in conservatories and moved outside when frosts have passed. The scented species are particularly suitable for indoor use.

Propagation is either from seed or from summer cuttings. In the open, a light pruning of the flowering stems is all that is required; under glass, they can be pruned harder, after flowering, to keep them compact.

Boronia crenulata derives its name from the crenate margins to its aromatic leaves. It is a small bush, 50cm to a metre (1½ to 3ft) high, with deep rosy pink flowers, which have stripes of a deeper colour on the outside.

B. floribunda is a very floriferous plant, covered with pale pink or near-white flowers. The leaves are aromatic when crushed.

B. heterophylla has highly scented, bell-shaped flowers, the colour of which is quite variable around a deep rosy pink base. The leaves are also aromatic.

B. megastima is different from most of the others, with flowers that are a dark purplish brown on the outside and a yellowish green on the inside. Both the flowers and the leaves are scented, the former having a very powerful and sweet perfume.

B. serrulata is a small bush, up to a metre (3ft) high. This species also has fragrant flowers, in this case of a deep rose-pink colour. The leaves have a reddish tinge towards the edge and are aromatic if crushed.

Bougainvillea

BOUGAINVILLEA

THESE ARE EXTREMELY COLOURFUL climbers with which many people have fallen in love while on holiday in the sun. The sun is the key to these plants; they are decidedly tender and can only be grown in frost-free areas. However, more people now own conservatories and these make an excellent place in which to over-winter bougainvilleas, as long as the temperature does not drop below 8°C (46°F). The temperature should be raised a few degrees in spring to bring the plants into growth. Bougainvilleas can be grown in large tubs or in beds built into the conservatory. The colour comes not from the petals but from the leafy bracts that surround the flower. These are borne for a very long season, often completely overpowering the foliage.

Bougainvilleas are happy in any fertile soil and though they like the full sun they will take a little shade. They can be trained into a variety of shapes, including arches or standards, or even hedges, if your conservatory needs a room divider.

Propagation is from heeled summer cuttings. Bougainvilleas can grow very big if left to their own devices, and pruning is

Bougainvillea
Zone 10

Bougainvillea × *buttiana* 'APPLE BLOSSOM'

undertaken in early spring, when lateral spurs are cut back almost to the main stems.

B. × *buttiana*, a hybrid between *B. glabra* and *B. peruviana*, is the commonest species in cultivation. There are a large number of cultivars, including 'APPLE BLOSSOM', with white bracts tinged with pink, and 'BRILLIANCE', which includes several shades of red, all present at the same time.

B. spectabilis has a dense growth and hairy leaves. It also has more spines than the other species. The bracts are found in a range of pinks and reds.

Bougainvillea spectabilis

Buddleia

BUTTERFLY BUSH

THIS WELL-KNOWN OPEN SHRUB is evocative of hot summer days and butterflies. The common forms feature long, fragrant spikes of mauve and purple flowers, but there are also species that produce round globes of yellow or orange. Buddleias are summer and autumn flowering, and the leaves are usually grey and felted.

These are plants of the sun, although they will take a little light shade. They grow best in good, rich soil but are fairly tolerant of poorer soils, even growing on chalk cliffs in disused quarries. They are reasonably hardy (−12°C;

Buddleia
Zone 7

Buddleia alternifolia

10°F) and if cut down by the frosts will generally regenerate from the base. In spite of regular pruning they will soon reach 10-15ft (3-4m) high.

The soft grey leaves and pastel colours of the flowers make this an ideal plant for the mixed border as a background for other medium-height, soft-coloured plants. *B. davidii* fits in particularly well with the concept of an herbaceous border as it is rigorously cut back each year. The darker purples and reds are more difficult to accommodate but they can suit a strongly-coloured border. Buddleias look well together in small groups in a shrub border or as a specimen clump.

Propagation is easy, from cuttings in late summer or from seed, though seed cannot be relied on to produce true plants from named forms. Pruning falls into two groups: those species that flower on new wood should be cut back to within a few inches of the previous year's growth in the spring. Those that flower on old wood should be lightly pruned after flowering to remove some of the older stems.

There are several species and cultivars available, the commonest being *B. davidii*, from China. This has blue to mauve flowers and should be pruned back hard, nearly to the old wood, in the spring. It has a large number of interesting varieties, ranging from the dark purple 'BLACK KNIGHT' and the rich crimson

'BORDER BEAUTY' to the whites, 'WHITE BOU-QUET' and 'WHITE PROFUSION'. Other cultivars worth growing include 'NANHO ALBA' (white), 'PEACE' (white), 'EMPIRE BLUE' (blue), 'CHARM-ING' (pink), 'FASCINATING' (pink), 'AMPLISSIMA' (mauve), 'ORCHID BEAUTY' (mauve), 'HARLE-QUIN' (purple), 'OPERA' (deep purple), and 'ROYAL RED' (deep purple).

B. alternifolia has graceful arching branches with clusters of fragrant lilac flowers clothing the ends of the branches. It is one of the hardiest species and will form a small tree suitable for planting in a lawn. Pruning should be confined to removing some of the old wood after flowering.

B. colvilei has deep rose flowers in long spikes and its foliage is darker than that of most other buddleias. It is not so hardy as *B. davidii*, but there are some interesting cultivars, including 'KEWENSIS', which has dark red flowers. This species should be pruned after flowering by removing some of the old wood.

B. crispa has rounder, shorter spikes of lilac flowers, with orange in their throats. The stems are clothed with a dense white felt. Again, some of the old wood should be removed after flowering.

B. fallowiana has very fragrant lavender flowers on white woolly stems. This is a tender shrub, not taking temperatures much below freezing, and it should thus be given a sheltered

Buddleia globosa

Buddleia fallowiana

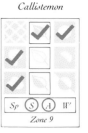

Callistemon

Sp (S) (A) W'
Zone 9

cultivars. Gardeners in areas too cold to grow them safely outside are now doing so in greenhouses and, increasingly, in conservatories.

The bottle brush of the name is a flower spike in which the coloured stamens, sticking out like the bristles of the brush, play the important part, while the petals are small and almost insignificant. The flowers are followed by woody seed capsules, which persist on the stem for several years. Both these and the flowers are sought after by flower arrangers. The evergreen leaves are lanceolate or willow-like in shape and a dull green in colour. Callistemons are quite quick growing and will reach about 3m (10ft) in favourable conditions. Several species will take a light frost, but not below −4 to −5°C (25 to 23°F).

Bottle brushes grow in moist, often swampy, land in the wild, but they will grow in quite dry areas in cultivation as long as the soil is reasonably moisture retentive. As they are tender they can only be grown outside in milder areas, and even here it is advisable to give them the protection of a warm wall.

This is a spectacular shrub and should be treated as a specimen plant. Its association with other plants is restricted by its need for wall protection. The fiery, hot reds are difficult to mix and really need softer colours as companions. The light airiness of *Alchemilla*

position. There is also a white form, 'ALBA'.

B. globosa is very different to the above. Its yellow-orange flowers, which appear earlier than those of some of the other buddleias, are in rounded balls, and it has attractive dark green foliage that is partially evergreen. Some of the old wood should be removed immediately after flowering. This is one of the hardiest species (−15°C; 5°F).

B. × *weyeriana* is similar to *B. globosa*, with balls of yellow-orange flowers, in this case sometimes suffused with lilac. In many ways this is a more subtle plant than *B. globosa*, of which it is a cross with *B. davidii*. It inherits *B. globosa*'s hardiness.

Callistemon

AUSTRALIAN BOTTLE BRUSH

THE MEMBERS OF THIS spectacular genus of trees and shrubs from Australia live up to their common name by looking just like sets of brightly coloured bottle brushes. As is so common with a lot of the more exotic-looking shrubs, callistemons have the drawback of being tender in cool climates. They make excellent indoor plants, however, and there is an ever-increasing list of available species and

Callistemon rigidus

mollis might have just the right effect, particularly as it will enhance the bright reds even more.

Propagation is from seed or cuttings taken in summer. Not much pruning is required except what is necessary to keep the plant tidy or, while it is becoming established, to encourage a tree-like growth.

C. citrinus is one of the hardiest species. It has a bright crimson spike, about 10cm (4in) long, and there is a commonly available cultivar, 'SPLENDENS', that has an even greater degree of brilliance. The "citrinus" of the Latin name comes from the lemon fragrance that the leaves emit when crushed.

C. rigidus has red flowers and its availability must be an indication of its hardiness.

C. salignus has different forms, with either creamy or pink stamens, forming 5-7cm (2-3in) flower spikes. It is reasonably hardy. It is not so spectacular as *C. citrinus* but it is easier to associate with other plants.

C. sibieri, the Alpine Bottle Brush, takes colder weather quite well, as its name implies. It has much smaller flower spikes than the others described here and they are yellow, but its reputation for hardiness makes it worth considering.

C. viminalis, Weeping Bottle Brush is a weeping small tree. It grows up to 6m (20ft) and is covered with scarlet flowers.

Calluna

Sp (S) A W
Zone 7

Callistemon citrinus

Calluna vulgaris 'DARKNESS'

Calluna

HEATHER; LING; SCOTCH HEATHER

THIS IS A MONOTYPIC genus that is so closely related to the heaths, *Erica*, that at first glance it just looks like another member of that group. Calluna is a low growing shrub, rarely reaching much above 30cm (1ft) or so in height. The branches are covered with narrow evergreen leaves and, during the summer, with bell-shaped flowers of purple, pink or white. It is fairly hardy, taking temperatures down to $-15°C$ (5°F).

Like all the ericaceous plants, this is a lime hater and cannot be grown on alkaline soils. It prefers full sun but will take a little shade.

Heathers make very good ground cover, but can become very monotonous if used too liberally. They can be of advantage as temporary fillings between such plants as rhododendrons, which will later grow to fill the space. The variation in leaf colour offers a means of lightening some areas, particularly in front of dark conifers.

Heathers can be propagated easily from cuttings taken in the summer. Pruning is restricted to a light trim in the spring to keep them in shape and promote new growth.

There is only one species in this genus, *Calluna vulgaris*, but there is a large number of

Calluna vulgaris 'H E BEALE'

CAMELLIA

CAMELLIAS MUST BE ONE of the greatest joys of spring; many people consider it to be perfection. The simplicity and purity of the flowers framed against the glossy green leaves can take the breath away, though this perfection is somewhat tarnished in a wet spring when the flowers are fading and appear as a soggy brown mess against the same glossy leaves. Romanticism is not born of such memories, however, and the plant's just reputation belongs to its former image.

It was once considered tender, but now there are many relatively hardy cultivars available in a large range of colours, from pure white through pinks to dark red. The shape varies from single and semi-double to full double flowers.

Camellias are usually sited as specimen plants because they flower too early to make it practical to associate them with other flowers, but their glossy evergreen foliage makes them an ideal background during the rest of the year for many other plants. Clear-coloured flowers look particularly good in front of them; plants such as the gleaming white *Zantedeschia* or the bright red monardas. Camellias make good plants for tubs that can be moved around, but they must be rigorously

Zone 8

cultivars from which to choose.

C.v. alba, which has white flowers in summer, is the common White Heather. It has a double form, 'ALBA PLENA'.

'AUREA' has a golden foliage and purple flowers in summer.

'CUPREA' has mauve flowers in summer, but it is the golden foliage that turns orange in the autumn and winter that is of interest.

'DARKNESS' has pink-purple flowers in autumn.

'GOLDEN FEATHER', as its name implies, has golden foliage darkening in autumn. The flowers appear in summer and are pink.

'H.E. BEALE' is a double-flowered form that appears lilac-pink in the autumn.

'KINLOCHRUEL' has white double flowers in the late summer.

'ROBERT CHAPMAN' is another autumn flowerer, this time a deep pink. The leaves are red-tinted in winter.

'SILVER QUEEN' is a mauve autumn flowerer. Its charm lies in the silvery foliage.

'SUNSET' has pink flowers but it is the yellow-orange foliage that is the most attractive feature, particularly as this deepens in colour, developing red tints in the winter.

There are many, many more to choose from and, as with other popular plants, a visit to a garden that specializes in them will be of advantage when it comes to making a choice.

Camellia japonica 'ADOLPHE AUDUSSON'

Camellia japonica 'NOBLISSIMA'

Camellia × *williamsii* 'J C WILLIAMS'

watered, particularly in hot weather. Conservatories also offer camellias a good home, where they will flower continually for several months, protected from the worst of the weather.

It is best to plant camellias in an acid, peaty soil as they are unhappy in alkaline conditions. Siting is crucial because the flower buds are often covered in frost and a sudden thawing by warm sun will ruin them; instead, they must defrost slowly. Indeed, any sudden variation in conditions can spell disaster, so they make ideal plants for filling the gaps on a

shady wall, where they will be sheltered from cold winds and early-morning winter sun.

Propagation is from cuttings taken in the summer. No pruning is necessary except for general tidying of the plant.

The number of camellia cultivars runs into the hundreds. Many of these are bred for the specialist grower and collector, but even so there is still a great choice available to other gardeners. Ultimately the best thing is to buy the plants in flower and choose the ones that most appeal to you.

Some of the best and most well known are *C.* × *williamsii* hybrids, for example the classic 'DONATION', with pink, semi-double flowers, or the single pink 'J.C. WILLIAMS'. 'MARY

Camellia 'DONATION'

CHRISTIAN' is another, darker pink.

One of the parents of *C.* × *williamsii* is *C. japonica*, which has produced many wonderful cultivars, all of them fairly hardy (−10°C; 14°F). 'ADOLPHE AUDUSSON' is one of the most popular, with its blood-red, semi-double flowers. 'NOBILISSIMA' is a good white form and makes its appearance early in the season.

The list could go on for many more pages, but the best thing is to go and choose for yourself.

Carpenteria californica

Carpenteria

CARPENTERIA

THIS IS A MONOTYPIC genus, that is to say there is only one species, *Carpenteria californica*. This should not deter anyone, because in this case one is plenty enough. If you like white flowers, this is one of those shrubs that should be on your shopping list. In the summer, it has beautiful pure white, saucer-shaped flowers, in the centre of which is a boss of yellow stamens. Carpenteria is evergreen, but many of the lanceolate leaves are browned during most winters, and if possible it should be protected from cold winds. It is not very hardy, standing frosts down to about −5°C (23°F); anything below that will cut the plant to the ground and it will take a couple of seasons before the plant flowers properly again. If a carpenteria survives the frosts for any number of years it will reach up to 3m (10ft).

It will tolerate a wide range of soils, but because of its tender nature it is best sited against a wall and in a position where it will receive the maximum possible sunlight.

Carpenteria makes a good specimen shrub and can be made a fine focal point among other colours or used as part of a white or white and silver garden.

Propagation can take place either from seed or from cuttings taken in summer, though seed can produce some inferior plants that should be ruthlessly discarded. Pruning is restricted to removing some of the old growth to prompt new shoots. Carpenteria will regenerate well from either a heavy pruning or frost attack, but since the flowers appear on old wood it will take a while to settle down again.

There only seems to be one variety other than the type-plant which might be available and this is 'LADHAM'S VARIETY', which is a profuse flowerer with larger blooms.

Carpenteria

Sp (*S*) *A* *W*
Zone 9

Caryopteris

CARYOPTERIS

THE SPECIFIC NAME, *Caryopteris* × *clandonensis*, is a rather clumsy name for a very beautiful bush that comes into flower in autumn, after most other shrubs have given up. There are several species in this genus but *clandonensis* is the only one that is generally available. This is a shrub with fine, grey, lanceolate leaves and light or bright blue flowers, the whole having a wonderful ethereal feeling. Indeed one of its names is Blue Mist Bush.

Some people feel that it is not very hardy, and it is susceptible to cold winds, but I have had it down to −15°C (5°F) without any ill-effects. It reaches its full height of a metre

Caryopteris

Sp *S* (*A*) *W*
Zone 7

Caryopteris × clandonensis

(3ft) very quickly and is not at all fussy about soil, growing virtually anywhere as long as it has plenty of sun.

It always gives me the greatest of pleasure to see this bush in autumn – it blends in so well with other blues, soft pinks or mauves. As a contrast, it also looks striking with yellows such as hypericums. Its short stature and misty quality means that it should be positioned towards the front of a border. I recollect that Christopher Lloyd once recommended raising plants from cuttings and using them as bedding plants, and this would certainly make an interesting display.

As intimated, propagation is from cuttings which, if taken in summer, take readily. *Caryopteris* × *clandonensis* should be cut right back each spring.

Ceonothus

Sp S A W
Zone 7

Ceanothus

CALIFORNIAN LILAC

THIS IS A VERY interesting group of shrubs because they belong to the small number that have blue flowers. In the case of ceanothus the colours run the whole range from pale to dark blue. The flowers themselves are very small, but since they appear in large clusters that cover the whole bush they give the impression

Ceanothus arboreus 'TREWITHEN BLUE'

Ceanothus dentatus

of a fluffy mass of pure blue with a few spaces for the green leaves to peep through. There are two types: evergreen, with small, tight leaves, and deciduous, with larger leaves and a more open habit. Hardiness is much debated. Certainly I have known plants to come through severe winters with temperatures down to −14°C (6°F). They lost their leaves but these reappeared and the plants flowered, although perhaps not so well as normal. It should be added that these particular plants lie against a south wall, which is the recommended position. Against a wall many ceanothuses can be very vigorous and rapidly grow to 4m (13ft) or more – a sight worth seeing when they are in flower.

They are quite tolerant to a range of soils, but dislike pure chalk. In colder districts they should have the protection of a wall; elsewhere they can grow as specimen bushes.

The range of blues available allows a form to be chosen which will allow it to fit into a variety of colour schemes, but ceanothuses fit particularly well into soft pastel schemes, where they tone with other blues and pinks.

Propagation should be from cuttings taken with a heel in late summer. Pruning should be undertaken with caution, as ceanothus does not readily break from old wood. It is possible to shear off the current year's growth after flower, but any deeper incisions are likely to result in ugly brown areas of stubs and stems, particularly at the base. These should be removed from sight by positioning another plant in front.

C. arboreus 'TREWITHEN BLUE' is one of the more vigorous of the evergreens, with sky blue, scented flowers.

C. 'AUTUMNAL BLUE' is an evergreen, with large, rich blue clusters of flowers, and it is a useful late flowerer.

C. × delilianus 'GLOIRE DE VERSAILLES' is

Ceanothus thyrsiflorus

the most popular of the deciduous varieties. This is also quite vigorous and has large loose panicles of pale blue flowers in the latter part of the summer. It is closely related to 'TOPAZ', which has much deeper blue flowers, while 'MARIE SIMON' has, unusually, rose-pink ones.

C. dentatus and *C. impressus* both have small evergreen leaves and bright blue flowers and make very good wall shrubs.

C. thyrsiflorus is another evergreen, but with larger leaves and pale blue flowers. It has a popular prostrate form, 'REPENS', which is very useful in a mixed border. This is only about a metre (3ft) high and has a spread of at least twice that.

Ceratostigma willmottianum

Ceratostigma

SHRUBBY PLUMBAGO

HAVING MENTIONED THE PAUCITY of blue-flowered shrubs, this is the third in a row, but here the line ends for a while. Shrubby plumbago is a small group of species of which *C. willmottianum*, Miss Willmott's Plumbago, is the most important for the garden. This has deep blue flowers, resembling small periwinkles in shape, from the end of the summer and into autumn. The dark green foliage sets off these flowers well. *C. willmottianum* is deciduous and, before they drop, the leaves turn to a good autumn colour of orange and red. The plant reaches a height of about a metre (3ft) and is reasonably hardy, taking temperatures to below −10°C (14°F).

The shrub is quite happy in a wide variety of soils, including chalky ones. It must, however, have full sun.

The somewhat herbaceous quality in its appearance means that it looks appropriate in either a mixed or herbaceous border. In spite of its bright blue flowers, *C. willmottianum* looks attractive with quite a range of colours and will even take contrasting yellows, such as hypericum, as neighbours.

Propagation is easy, from softwood cuttings taken in summer. Pruning is a bit more of a problem as there are two schools of thought:

Ceratostigma

Sp (S) (A) *W*
Zone 8

Chaenomeles × *superba* 'NICOLINE'

Chaenomeles × *superba* 'KNAP HILL SCARLET'

some gardeners prune back to almost ground level each year, but I incline to the school that only takes out the dead wood after a hard winter and generally keeps the plant tidy. Flowering will start much earlier if the bush does not have to grow afresh each year.

Chaenomeles

Chaenomeles

		✓
✓	✓
✓		✓
Sp	S A W
Zone 6	

ORNAMENTAL QUINCE, JAPONICA

THIS IS A VERY HARDY SHRUB that produces masses of waxy flowers, resembling apple blossoms in shape. These are tightly clustered to the bare branches before the leaves emerge and range in colour from orangey red to rich dark red, pinks and pure white. The pear-shaped fruit that appears in autumn is also quite spectacular. On a wall, the shrub will grow up to 3m (10ft), but it can be easily pruned and kept to any height that is desired.

There are generally no problems with the type of soil it requires, and it is likewise quite happy in either sun or shade.

Ornamental quince can be used as a free-standing shrub, but I remember it from my childhood as a wall shrub and have thus preferred it in that situation ever since. In any case, it is useful in that position as it can be

grown on a north wall, where few brightly-coloured shrubs will flourish. I also enjoy it on an east or west wall, where the low spring sun will bring out the glow in the rich reds. It can be trained flat against a wall, especially where there is little room between the wall and a path. In this kind of position there is little with which you can associate it, although there would be room for aubrieta to climb around its feet.

Ornamental quince is normally propagated from semi-ripe cuttings in summer. Pruning is a harsh regime of cutting out all the previous year's growth after the shrub has

Chaenomeles japonica

flowered. In doing this, of course, the majority of the autumn's fruit is lost, so it might be sensible to be selective and leave a few old flowering stems. Without any yearly pruning, however, it becomes straggly.

There are three species: *C. japonica*, *C. speciosa* and *C. × superba*, none of which is common in its own right, though all are found in a wide array of cultivars.

C. speciosa has worthwhile varieties in 'NIVALIS' (white), 'SIMONII' (excellent deep red), 'SNOW' (pure white) and 'UMBILICATA' (deep pink).

C. × superba includes the magnificent form 'CRIMSON AND GOLD', with its bright crimson flowers, each with a central boss of golden stamens. Other good forms are 'KNAP HILL SCARLET' (prolific scarlet flowers), 'NICO-LINE' (red), 'PINK LADY' (deep pink) and 'ROWALLANE' (bright crimson).

Chimonanthus

WINTERSWEET

THIS IS A SHRUB that would be of little importance if it were not for the fragrant flowers that it produces in the winter months, when such plants are most welcome. The flowers are held in bunches, tight to the branch, long before the leaves are produced, and have two sets of waxy petals, those on the outside being a pale yellow and those on the inside purple. This plant takes several years to settle down before it produces flowers, so patience is essential if you are not to become bored with the wait. It is tolerably hardy (−10°C; 14°F) and grows to about 2.5m (8ft) if the frost has not cut it back.

Wintersweet is quite happy on most soils and although it prefers full sun, it will tolerate a little bit of shade.

This is a plant for the winter only and it is difficult to find the ideal position: it should be near a path for appreciation in the winter, preferably in full sun for its wellbeing, but tucked out of sight, or at least masked by more interesting plants, in the summer. It is possible to grow a climber through it, either a delicate

Chimonanthus praecox

Chimonanthus

Sp · S · A · (W)
Zone 8

plant, such as *Clematis alpina*, or something much more brash and overpowering, such as nasturtiums.

Propagation is from cuttings in summer or from seed, though the latter will produce some worthless seedlings that will have to be kept a number of years before this quality becomes apparent.

There is only one species in general cultivation, *Chimonanthus praecox*. This has two popular cultivars: 'GRANDIFLORUS', with larger flowers but less scent, and 'LUTEUS', which is all yellow, being without the purple colouring on the inner petals.

Choisya

MEXICAN ORANGE

THIS WONDERFUL SHRUB REALLY earns its keep – it has masses of waxy, white flowers at the merging of spring and summer and, if the summer has been reasonably hot and sunny, a second flush of flowers in autumn. These flowers are highly scented and the fragrance pervades the garden. The evergreen leaves are a glossy green and are held like three fingers. If crushed they are also aromatic. The plant is quite hardy (−12°C; 10°F), and if cut back by frost it will quickly regenerate. It quickly grows to about 3m (6ft) or more.

Choisya

Sp · S · A · W
Zone 7

Choisya ternata

year to encourage new growth, especially as the plant regenerates so readily. The branches are brittle and can easily be damaged, particularly by snow, in which case they should be tidied up.

The one species that has been grown for many years is *Choisya ternata*. This has one cultivar widely available, 'SUNDANCE', which has yellow foliage, but which somehow lacks the authority of the green type-plant.

This is often thought to be a monotypic genus, but there are several other species, one of which, *C. arizonica*, is beginning to appear at shows and to become available.

Cistus

Choisya is not at all fussy about soils or about siting, but it will flower better in full sun.

This is a very useful shrub, even for the small garden. Being evergreen, it can be used as a screen at the same time as acting as a background to other plants, either herbaceous or shrubby. It is a good architectural plant for a border, giving it solid form and shape, and its glossy leaves and white flowers will take most colours as companions.

Propagation is easy from cuttings taken in summer. No pruning is necessary, but it is a good idea to remove some of the old wood each

Cistus

ROCK ROSE

CISTUS COME FROM THE hot lands around the Mediterranean, as the most casual glance at the shrub in flower would indicate. The flowers are rose-shaped and appear to be made of tissue paper – they seem to cry out for the bright Mediterranean sun. They are very fleeting, lasting only the day, sometimes only a few hours, but they are followed by new flowers, opening day after day throughout the summer. Although some of the colours are quite dark they all have the same soft

Choisya arizonica

Cistus ladinifer

Sp (S) A W
Zone 7

Cistus × aguilari

Cistus × purpureus

appearance that characterizes this plant. Many have a dark purple, chocolate or yellow patch at the base of each petal. There is a great range of colours available, from white through pink to crimson. The medium-sized leaves are green or grey and some people find them rather dull, though certain species have leaves that are deliciously aromatic when wet. There is quite a variation in height and some types will grow up to 2m (6ft).

Hardiness is debatable, as it is with so many plants. Coming from Mediterranean regions, rock roses are naturally expected to be tender, as indeed some undoubtedly are, but many have come through fairly severe winters, taking for example −14°C (7°F) in my garden. They are truly wonderful plants to have in the garden, and even if their hardiness is in doubt it is well worth taking the risk. Most species are salt tolerant and make good seaside plants.

Rock roses have a wide tolerance of soils, provided that they are well drained. A position in full sun is essential, both for the plant and for its appreciation.

They are marvellous for the mixed border, and look particularly good when mixed with other soft colours, such as mauves, pinks, purples and the lighter blues.

Propagation is from softwood cuttings in summer. Alternatively they grow readily

from seed, but there is no guarantee that a seedling will have the same colouring as its parent. Restrict pruning to tidying up the plant and removing any dead wood.

C. × aguilari is best known for the variety 'MACULATUS'. This has large flowers with a crimson blotch at the base of each petal. *C. × cyprius* is very similar in flower, but has shiny green leaves.

C. × corbariense is one of the most widely available. This has white flowers with yellow centres, and light green foliage.

C. ladinifer is one of the most popular

Cistus albidus

species. This also has white flowers with a deep red, almost chocolate blotch at the base of the petals.

C. laurifolius is one of the hardiest species. It has white flowers with a touch of yellow at the base of the petals.

C. × purpureus is a good rose pink with a dark basal blotch and grey-green leaves and it is a widely available and popular plant. One of its varieties, 'BETTY TAUDEVIN', is particularly good, with bright flowers.

Clematis cirrhosa balearica

Clematis 'NELLY MOSER'

Clematis

Zone 5

Clematis

CLEMATIS

CAN THERE BE ANY garden worthy of the name that does not have a clematis in it? This is one of the finest groups of plants ever to be introduced. It is almost possible to go right through the year with one or other of the clematis in flower – even in winter, *C. cirrhosa* var. *balearica* will start to flower, particularly if grown in a conservatory. The majority are woody climbing plants, although there are a few which are herbaceous and die back each year. The flowers vary from almost insignificant wisps to large, full-blown cartwheels. The colours cover a large part of the spectrum between blue and red.

Yellow is one of the problem colours, because although there are yellow varieties of the smaller species, true yellow has not yet appeared in the bigger forms, and it is these bigger forms – particularly the blues, mauves and purples – that make such spectacular splashes of colour over walls, trellises and old (or new) trees. But the intermediate-sized *viticella* and *montana* types also make an amazing sight, and the latter in particular do a remarkably good job of covering up eyesores.

The above all have the conventional flat-faced flowers, but there are also species with bell-shaped flowers or starry strap petals. Here, the flowers are much smaller and these species are on the whole bought by the collector, rather than the general gardener. (There is no reason why this should be so except that they are less well known.)

Most clematis are rampant climbers and will easily climb up to 3m (10ft) or often even more, but some of the New Zealand green-flowered species that have recently been introduced into cultivation reach only 30cm (1ft) or less and are very dainty, with attractive seed heads.

Clematis are happy with most soils. It is often said that they need limy or chalky soils to do their best but you should take little notice of this; there are many fine specimens that have never seen a hint of chalk or lime. Many are plants of the sun and look best in full sunlight provided their roots are kept cool and out of the sun. The traditional way of coping with this is by placing large stones around the plant, but a good mulching of manure or compost with another plant in front to cast shade around the base of the clematis is sufficient. Although they are plants of the sun, it must be admitted that many of them will thrive equally well in shade, indeed some varieties are better so situated to prevent the sun bleaching the colour from the petals.

For most clematis in cultivation, hardiness is not much of a problem in any area. What can be a problem in the initial stages is wilt, when the young plant will suddenly keel over. There is no real cure for this, but if the plant has been planted deeply enough, it will normally produce growth again the following year. Once past infancy, this problem usually disappears. Clematis need cool roots, so it is a wise precaution to mulch heavily.

Where to plant the clematis? Everywhere! They make excellent screens growing up trellises. Similarly they make a superb background to a border, or climbing up wigwams of poles they make a fine feature in the border itself. They can be grown through old trees that are past their prime or through shrubs that have nothing to contribute during the clematis' flowering season. In wilder gardens they can be left to ramp wherever they

Clematis jackmanii

Clematis montana 'GRANDIFLORA'

please. This sounds a bit hit or miss, but plants have a happy knack of putting themselves where they look best. Something that often puzzles me with clematis is why, given the size and brightness of individual flowers and the sheer volume of colour of the massed blooms, they rarely seem garish and seldom fail to fit into the scheme of things, whatever that scheme may be.

Propagation seems a bit of a mystery to some people, but most clematis come readily from cuttings taken in midsummer. Pruning is not quite so simple, as there are three basic methods depending on the plant. Some, mainly the *montana* types, require no pruning, save the removal of dead wood. Those that flower on new wood should be cut back to a good pair of buds as close to the ground as possible. For those that flower on old wood, dead and weak growths should be removed and the remainder cut back to the first pair of strong buds. The problem is to know which clematis belongs to each category. Nothing should go wrong if you make a mistake, the worst will be that you will miss a flowering season, but if you ask your supplier he should be able to tell you; the moral being always to use reliable suppliers.

There are some groups of plants, such as clematis, roses and rhododendrons, that are so large and full of good plants that it is impossible to know where to begin and where to end in describing their members. It cannot be emphasized enough that ultimately it comes down very much to personal choice and the reader is exhorted to go and see the plants in flower in gardens, or in nurseries and garden centres, and then make a choice. The list that follows is but a brief selection of personal favourites.

Starting with the large-flowered varieties, 'ELSA SPÄTH', also called 'XERXES', is a good lavender blue with a purple boss of stamens. It is large (20cm; 8in across) and lasts very well from late spring. *C. jackmanii*, with its 15cm (6in) purple flowers, has long been one of the most popular clematis. Its form 'SUPERBA' has even richer colour and fuller petals. Both have green stamens and flower during the summer. The finest of the whites is 'MARIE BOISSELOT' or 'MADAME LE COULTRE' as she is sometimes known. The flowers, which can be up to 20cm (8in) across, are pure white, with yellow stamens. Another great favourite has always been 'NELLY MOSER', which has great 23cm (9in) flowers in a very pale mauvy pink with a dark, almost carmine, stripe down the centre of the petal. This is a good plant for a shady position, such as a north wall. Reds are not quite so successful, but 'VILLE DE LYON' is one of the best, with deep carmine flowers and yellow stamens. There are so many more that ought to be described but space only allows

mention of 'THE PRESIDENT' (blue), 'PERLE D'AZUR' (light blue), 'MRS HOPE' (pale blue) and 'NIOBE' (red).

A description of the smaller-flowered varieties must start with *C. montana*, a common sight in early summer, with its mass of pink or white flowers. 'ELIZABETH' is a good pink form with a lovely vanilla perfume. 'RUBENS' is a darker pink form with bronzy foliage, while 'ALBA' is a vigorous white form. A similar plant that is one of my favourites is *C. chrysocoma* with its delicate pink flowers and downy, bronze foliage. The *viticella* group is another favourite, particularly the rich velvet red of 'ROYAL VELOURS'. *C. viticella* itself is well worth growing for its nodding purple flowers.

Some of the species are commonly available and are delightful plants to see in a garden, although they may not be quite so spectacular as some of the larger varieties. *Clematis orientalis*, the Orange Peel Clematis, has delicate filigree foliage and yellow flowers, composed of four thick yellow petals, resembling peel. *C. tangutica* and *C.* 'BILL MACKENZIE' are somewhat similar but have the added advantage of spectacular silky seedheads.

There are many more to explore but here I must stop and let the reader find his or her own way.

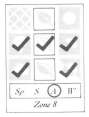

Clerodendrum

Clematis tangutica

Clerodendrum

CLERODENDRUM

THESE TREES AND SHRUBS are useful because of their late flowering nature and their delicious scent. There are only two species of interest, one with clusters of rose-pink flowers and the other white. Both species flower in the autumn and are followed by blue fruit that can persist into winter. Both also have foliage that, if crushed, has a rather nasty odour, and they also have a nasty habit of producing suckers. Clerodendrum grows to a nice dense bush but can be a nuisance in a border. It is quite hardy, taking temperatures down to −10°C (14°F) or so, and though it will often be cut back by frost it will regenerate.

Clerodendrum bungei

Both species will tolerate any soil and prefer light shade, though they will accept full sun if the soil is sufficiently rich and moist.

They are best as specimen shrubs or in a shrubbery: in any other situation the suckers can be a nuisance.

Propagation is readily achieved by removing rooted suckers from around the plant. Pruning is restricted to the removal of dead or weak growth and control of the suckers.

Clerodendrum bungei is a small bush of up to a metre (3ft) in good conditions. It has rounded clusters of rose-pink flowers and large heart-shaped leaves.

C. trichotomum has loose clusters of white flowers held in red calyces. The leaves are ovate. There is a form *fargesii* that has purple foliage when young and paler calyces.

Convolvulus

CONVOLVULUS

MOST PEOPLE ARE ONLY aware of convolvulus as the bindweed that grows as a persistent weed and seems impossible to remove from the garden. There are, however, several other members of the genus, some of which are as tenacious as bindweed while others are superb small shrubs. Only a couple will be mentioned but both have the typical funnel-shaped flowers of the genus and both are unfortunately somewhat tender, −5°C (23°F), though they are small enough to be grown in tubs and moved inside for the winter or to be grown each year from cuttings.

Convolvulus cneorum is a very beautiful shrub with silver lanceolate leaves setting off pure white funnels that are sometimes ribbed on the reverse side with pink. It will stand a certain amount of frost if it is in a well-drained, sunny position, protected from cold winds (the wet is probably what it dislikes, rather than the cold). This plant can easily be grown from cuttings taken in summer. It is a choice plant that will look beautiful outside in a border or in a tub. In the border it combines delightfully with pinks right through to magenta.

The other plant is even smaller and more tender. *C. sabatius*, sometimes called *C. mauritanicus*, has charming soft-blue flowers set against a blue-green leaf. This species makes a small shrub only 30cm (1ft) tall that looks magnificent in small terracotta pots. Again, it can be propagated by cuttings.

Convolvulus

Sp (S) (A) W
Zone 9

Convolvulus sabatius

They are happy in all soils and many will even take to waterlogged conditions, which is not common among shrubs. Most prefer full sun but will take some shade.

Although this is primarily a book about flowering shrubs, the dogwoods exhibit other qualities that must be taken into account when choosing a site. For example, those with good bark colours should be placed where they can be seen in winter and where they will catch the low sun of that time of year, so that it can bring out the richness of their colour. Those with variegated leaves should be positioned where they will brighten up a dark corner, or where they will stand out against darker foliage. Those with white bracts also show to their best advantage against a green background contributed by other trees and shrubs.

Propagation from cuttings is very easy or, in the case of *C. canadensis*, it can take place from division. In the majority of species, pruning is not essential, except for tidying up, but in the case of *C. alba* the plant ought to be cut to the ground each spring before the foliage develops if you wish to retain the bark colour the following winter. If it is the flowers that are your main concern, then this species should also be left unpruned.

Let us look at those species that are renowned for their flowers. *Cornus canadensis* is a very low growing (15-20cm; 6-8in) shrub

Cornus florida 'RUBRA'

Cornus

CORNEL; DOGWOOD

THIS IS AN EXTREMELY valuable group of shrubs and trees as they contribute so much to the garden in all seasons of the year: flowers, foliage and bark are all of interest. The flowers themselves are usually almost insignificant but they often have white or pink bracts that make them look larger and more important. Dogwoods are hardy down to −15°C (5°F) or more, and heights vary between 15cm and 9m (6in and 30ft).

Cornus

Sp S A W
Zone 7

Cornus canadensis

Cornus kousa

Cornus nuttallii

Mention should be made of *Cornus alba* and *C. stolonifera*, sometimes *C. sericea*, both of which are grown principally for the colour of their winter bark; red in the case of the former and yellow-green in the latter case.

Corylopsis

Corylopsis

Zone 7

WINTER HAZEL

THIS IS RELATED TO English hazel and has similar leaves but has more open catkins, in the form of small chains of fragrant yellow flowers, appearing in the late winter or early spring. Its height varies from small bushes of a metre (3ft) to much taller shrubs of 4m (13ft) or so. All are reasonably hardy, withstanding frosts as low as −15°C (5°F), but the flowers may be damaged.

Winter hazels are not too keen on limy soils and grow better on neutral or acid ones. Light shade is preferred.

They need to be sited to feature their late winter flowering; for the rest of the year, their somewhat dull leaves just contribute as a background to other plants.

They may be propagated from softwood cuttings taken in summer. No pruning is required other than removing dead wood.

Corylopsis pauciflora has only three, but

that makes excellent ground cover, particularly in shady positions. The flower itself is insignificant but sits as a central boss in four white bracts, giving the impression of a much more substantial flower. It can be used to brighten up the area under shrubs and trees.

C. florida is much larger, a tree or large shrub up to 5m (16ft) tall. Here the bracts are also much bigger, and although the type-plant is white, many of the more interesting cultivars are pink. White forms include 'BARTON WHITE', 'CHEROKEE CHIEF', 'PENDULA', which has a weeping habit, and 'RAINBOW', which has a variegated leaf. Good pink forms include 'APPLE BLOSSOM', 'RUBRA' and 'SPRING SONG'.

C. kousa has larger, creamy white bracts that are extremely good for lighting up a dark spot. It prefers light shade. There are quite a number of varieties, of which the best known is the subspecies *C.k. chinensis*. This last has bracts that are more spectacular than those of the type-plant, covering the whole plant.

Cornus mas, Cornelian Cherry, has no bracts, but it has so many small yellow flowers in late winter or early spring, before the leaves appear, that it seems to be clothed in gold.

Cornus nuttallii, Pacific Dogwood, has large bracts, sometimes up to 15cm (6in) across, producing a spectacular display of dazzling white. Again, there are several forms available.

Corylopsis vietchiana

Corylopsis willmottiae

quite large, flowers in each raceme. These are a strong yellow and smell of cowslips. This plant normally grows no higher than 2m (6ft).

C. platypetala is a large shrub that is quite widely available and has pale yellow flowers, hanging in long tassels.

C. sinensis var. *sinensis* (or *C. willmottiae*) is a graceful shrub, with paler flowers in longer racemes than the above. It also has young purple leaves, the best colour being found in the spring leaves of the form 'SPRING PURPLE'.

C. spicata (Spike Winterhazel) is a medium-size shrub. It has pale green-yellow flowers with purple anthers.

C. veitchiana is another good variety with prominent red-brown anthers and foliage that is purple when it first appears.

Corylus

HAZEL

HAZEL MAKES AN ATTRACTIVE SHRUB and is a good hedging plant for the garden. The catkins are tight racemes of yellow male flowers and are followed by edible hazelnuts in autumn. The latter are produced by the insignificant female flowers, which are no more than a tuft of red stamens sticking out of a bud. The general shape of the shrub is erect, with slightly arching stems, reaching a height of 5m (17ft). Hazels are very hardy. They will grow in any soil and are happy in either full sun or shade, although they flower better in the light.

They should be positioned to achieve the maximum winter effect from the catkins, and they look particularly good against a large evergreen, such as holly, that will show the catkins up at even 200m (600ft). The leaves of most species are a bright green and are of no real significance, though they can be used as a screen or background for other shrubs: hazels produce nice dappled shade for anemones, hellebores, primroses and other woodland-loving plants. There are also varieties with purple or other decorative foliage.

Hazels can be propagated from seed or from rooted shoots taken from the base. No pruning is generally required except for the removal of dead wood and some of the older wood, to allow the production of new shoots.

The hedgerow hazel, *Corylus avellana*, is readily available. Various cultivars are also to be found, most notably 'CONTORTA', known as either the Corkscrew Hazel or Harry Lauder's Walking Stick. In this, the stems and branches are contorted into strange twisted shapes. 'AUREA' has softer green foliage, turning yellow with age; 'HETEROPHYLLA' has smaller, deep-lobed leaves.

Corylus avellana 'CONTORTA'

C. maxima is the filbert or cobnut, from which edible nuts are produced. The deep purple-leaved form 'PURPUREA' is grown for its decorative effect.

Cotinus

SMOKE BUSH; VENETIAN SUMACH

THESE ARE GOOD ALL-ROUND deciduous trees or shrubs for the garden. They are extremely attractive both in leaf and in flower; indeed, as happens with so many plants, the two complement each other. The flowers themselves are minute silken threads borne on large, loose panicles, giving the overall impression of the smoke in the plant's name. The deciduous foliage consists of simple rounded leaves in green or, in some cultivars, purple. Smoke bushes are hardy to most of our requirements, down to −15°C (4°F). The shrubs will grow up to 5m (16ft) or more, but when grown for foliage effects they are often pollarded each year, the new growth only reaching to a height of 2m (6ft).

Smoke bushes can be accommodated in any soil, but they can get coarse if the soil is too rich. Most prefer full sun, but the green-leaved varieties can put up with light shade.

Cotinus coggygria

Cotinus

Sp (S) A W

Zone 7

The green-leaved types have the best flowering forms and can make very good specimen plants, particularly in lawns. The purple forms are marvellous border plants, and can be used to make dramatic associations: they can, for example, cope with the fiery red of such plants as *Lobelia cardinalis*, with silver-leaved plants such as the artemisias or, better still, with grasses, which give good contrast to their shape. They are also a suitable shrub through which to grow clematis, though the choice of colour must be made carefully.

Propagation is by layering or from heeled cuttings taken in late summer. Generally smoke bushes need no pruning, but they should be pollarded regularly to promote a fresh supply of young growth with larger, darker leaves. This, of course, reduces flowering, so only those plants being grown for their foliage effect should be pollarded.

Cotinus coggygria (still sold as *Rhus cotinus* in some places) is the main species. In its natural form it has green leaves and pale pink puffs of flowers. 'FLAME' has green leaves that turn to a very fine orangey red in autumn. 'FOLIIS PURPUREIS' has purplish green leaves and is one of the older cultivars. This has been superseded in colour by 'ROYAL PURPLE', which has leaves of a very dark purple, ravishing with the setting sun behind them.

C. obovatus (or sometimes *C. americanus*) is

Cotinus coggygria 'ROYAL PURPLE'

the only other species in the genus. It is grown less widely than *C. coggygria*. The leaves are bigger than in its rival; they turn from a bronzy colour in early spring to green, ending the year with brilliant autumn tinting. The flower is again pink.

Crinodendron

Zone 9

Crinodendron

LANTERN TREE

THIS IS A SMALL GENUS of two species, of which both are in cultivation. They are evergreen shrubs or small trees with bright red or white lanterns hanging singly on long stalks from the branches in early summer. The flowers start to form in autumn and it is not until the following summer that they are eventually fully developed. The branches are also clothed with narrow leathery leaves.

Crinodendrons will grow up to 4m (13ft) if the frosts will allow them, but they are not all that hardy (−5°C; 23°F). They should be grown in lime-free soil in full sun.

Because of their spectacular flowers, crinodendrons make striking specimen shrubs, but they should be planted in a warm, protected position, preferably against a wall.

They can be propagated from half-ripe cuttings taken in summer. No pruning is required except that which is needed to keep the plant tidy.

Crinodendron hookeranum is the commonest of the two species. This has bright red lanterns and is sometimes known as *Tricuspidaria lanceolata*.

C. patagua (or *Tricuspidaria dependens*) flowers later, producing white lanterns that are smaller than those of *C. hookeranum* and slightly more open mouthed. It is the more tender of the two.

Crowea saligna

Crowea

Zone 10

Crowea

CROWEA

THIS IS A SMALL GENUS of shrubs native to Australia. They are particularly useful in that they bloom throughout the winter and into the spring, producing starry flowers that differ in shade from pink to purple. The bushes are evergreen, with narrow leaves that are aromatic when bruised. They are not hardy and should only be grown outside in frost-free areas, but they can be grown in a warm conservatory.

Crowea like a light sandy soil, with added humus, and prefer light shade.

Their habit of flowering during the winter and spring means that they are best

Crinodendron hookeranum

planted where this quality can be most appreciated. They are small enough to be grown in tubs or other containers that can be kept in a conservatory during cold weather and moved outside for the summer.

Propagation is from seed or semi-hardwood cuttings. No pruning is required except a light one after flowering, if this is needed to keep the plant compact.

Crowea angustifolia has pale pink or pinkish white flowers on a bush that grows up to a metre (3ft) high.

C. exalata is a small shrub growing up to 75cm (2½ft) with flowers that vary in colour from pale to dark rosy pink. This species has a long flowering season and its leaves are very aromatic.

C. saligna, Willow-leaved Crowea, grows up to a metre (3ft) high, and has rosy pink flowers. As both the Latin and Australian names imply, it has willow-shaped leaves, and these are aromatic when crushed.

Cytisus

BROOM

IN TERMS OF VALUE for money, the cytisus must provide more blooms for the square metre than most other plants. In spring it causes a tremendous splash of colour with its thousands of pea-like flowers. The colours are based mainly on yellow, but also include pinks and reds. The plants themselves vary in height from a few centimetres to 3m (10ft), with lots of thin green, arching stems. Not all carry leaves throughout the season, the colour and form being given by the green branches. When there are leaves they tend to be trifoliate and rather small. Although they are quite hardy, taking temperatures down to −12°C (10°F), cytisus are not very long-lived, but while they do live they are glorious, flowering from their first season.

On the whole they will tolerate any soil, the exception being *C. scoparius*, which is reluctant to grow on limy soils. They prefer sunny positions: they will grow in light shade,

Cytisus battandieri

but there is little reward in this for the gardener as the value of these plants lies in their flowers and these will be few in shady conditions.

The flowers make such a splash of colour that during their flowering time they are the focus of attention. It is difficult to associate other plants with broom, but a good idea is to position them with herbaceous plants. The broom will produce colour at a time when other plants are still growing and then merge into the background when the latter are in flower. Broom also looks very good in front of other green shrubs and certainly makes a

Cytisus

Sp S A W
Zone 8

Cytisus scoparius

Cytisus scoparius

distant focal point in larger gardens. As it is a short-lived plant, it is very useful to use as a temporary planting, say between two other shrubs that will eventually grow to cover the spot where the broom is planted.

Propagation can take place from seed, from softwood cuttings taken in summer, or from heeled cuttings in late summer. Seed should not be used from named cultivars as these will not come true. Pruning is not necessary for the smaller, compact varieties, but the rest should have all their flowering stems shortened back to the beginning of the new growth immediately after flowering. Cutting into old wood should be avoided. If the bushes are not trimmed they will soon get very lax and floppy.

Cytisus battandieri comes first in the list and yet it is the odd man out as it has solid panicles of flowers instead of individual flowers spread out along the branches. Its common name, Pineapple Broom, gives some idea of the shape of the flower head, which is a rich golden yellow. The leaves are also much larger than those of other species. This is a magnificent shrub, growing up to 5m (16ft) in favourable conditions. It is a bit on the tender side, only taking frosts down to about −5°C (23°F). It is widely available.

C. × *beanii* is a dwarf carpeting plant (60cm; 2ft) with golden yellow flowers.

C × *kewensis* is another procumbent plant of about the same height, this time with pale, creamy yellow flowers.

C. × *praecox* has a lot of interesting forms: 'ALBUS' is a good white; 'ALLGOLD', golden yellow; 'HOLLANDIA', rosy red, and 'ZEELAND-IA' is a bicoloured form, with pink and purplish flowers.

C. purpureus is very low growing and spreading. As its name implies it has purple flowers. The form 'ATROPURPUREUS' has even deeper coloured flowers.

C. scoparius is a native of western Europe although the various forms are now a long way from the original plant. *Scoparius* itself is widely available, but most of its hybrids and forms are

Cytisus 'LORD LAMBOURNE'

now given just by their cultivar name.

There are so many of these hybrids that the reader is again exhorted to go and look, before choosing. However, there is space to mention just a few, particularly the bicoloured forms: *andreanus* has bright red and yellow flowers; 'CORNISH CREAM' is two colours of pale yellow; 'DAISY HILL' is red and yellow, as is 'GOLDFINCH', and 'LORD LAMBOURNE' has pale yellow and dark red flowers.

Daphne

DAPHNE

THIS IS QUITE A LARGE GENUS of small, short-lived shrubs that are valuable for their sweet scent. The flowers are small and tubular, and

Daphne

Zone 8

Daphne × burkwoodii

are usually found in shades of pink, though there are some white variants and others that are naturally yellow. In many ways these are plants for the connoisseur. If they are just set at random in a border or shrubbery they can easily be overlooked, but when sited with care they are very attractive shrubs. They vary in stature from prostrate forms that grow no more than 2.5cm (1in) to plants that reach 1.5m (5ft).

Their hardiness varies, but the majority will take temperatures to −12°C (10°F) or more. Some people find daphnes difficult to keep alive, but if they are accepted as short-lived plants then they are worth growing.

They are tolerant of a wide range of soils, including chalk. Many are woodland plants and like to have a good loamy soil with plenty of the leaf mould that is found in that kind of situation. The majority prefer light shade but they will also take some sun.

Being small and perfumed they must be positioned where they can be seen and smelt, and at the same time they require a bit of light shading: near a path on the north side of a building would be an obvious choice. The winter-flowering species have no need for specific associations. Those that flower later fit well into a scheme of soft colours based on pinks, and their glossy, greenish leaves act as

a good foil to a range of plants. The smaller species are extremely good for the rock garden or for troughs and tubs.

Daphne can be propagated either from seed or from cuttings taken in the summer. No pruning is required except what is necessary to keep the plants tidy and remove any dead material.

Daphne × burkwoodii is the tallest of the species, reaching 1.5m (5ft). It is semi-evergreen, with soft, narrow leaves that form the perfect setting for the clusters of fragrant pink flowers that appear at the end of spring and last on into the early summer. It has two good forms, 'ALBERT BURKWOOD' and 'SOMER-SET' the former throwing up another sport, 'CAROL MACKIE'. The latter also has a variegated variant 'SOMERSET GOLD EDGE' that has a yellow edging to its leaves.

D. cneorum, Garland Flower, grows well as a rock garden plant. It has clusters of pink flowers that appear in the latter part of the spring. The plant itself is rather sprawling and although it reaches no more than 30cm (1ft) high, it spreads three times that across. It has some very lovely forms, certain of which are difficult to find. 'VARIEGATA', with variegated leaves, is the most easily obtainable.

D. mezereum, Mezereon, is one of the commonest of the daphnes. Its big advantage lies in the scented flowers that it produces in

Daphne mezereum

the winter. These are purple pink and appear tightly packed to the naked stems. There is a white form, 'ALBA'.

D. odora is a popular shrub, sporting highly scented pale pink flowers in spring, produced on large (1.5m; 5ft) evergreen stems. It also has a good white form 'ALBA'.

D. tangutica, which is widely available, again has pink flowers on evergreen branches, this time only 60cm (2ft) tall. This species produces good red berries later in the summer and takes full sun.

Davidia

Davidia

Sp S A W

Zone 8

Davidia

GHOST TREE; HANDKERCHIEF TREE

THIS MUST SURELY BE one of the most beautiful of the flowering trees. There is only one species in the genus, *Davidia involucrata*, but this is sufficient. The charm of this tree is not really the flower – this is only a ball of about 2cm (¾in) across – but the two white, papery bracts that surround them. These two bracts are of unequal size and look like handkerchiefs casually thrown onto the tree. In good specimens the whole tree is covered. The green leaves are quite large, ovate and with heavy veining, the undersides being felted.

Deutzia

Deutzia

Sp S A W

Zone 6

Davidia involucrata

The tree grows to about 12m (40ft) and is fairly hardy, taking temperatures down to −12°C (10°F), though it may die back in temperatures at the lower end of the scale. The only drawback to the handkerchief tree is that extreme patience is required – it does not flower until it is about 20 years old. Considering this fact, it is surprising that, although sizeable specimens are hard to find, the tree is available from specialist nurseries.

The soil should present no problem as it is fairly tolerant of most types. It is happy with sun or light shade.

The positioning of the tree is crucial. If, after twenty years, when it first flowers, you find that it is in the wrong place, it is a bit late to start again. It is truly a specimen tree and looks stunning against the blue sky or against the green of other, taller trees. They are wonderful trees for the twilight or for moonlit nights, when the white bracts appear quite ghostly.

They are propagated by layering branches from young plants. Initial pruning is required to promote a single-stemmed, tree-like shape, but little subsequent treatment is needed.

Only one form is available, *D.i. vilmoriniance*, which is similar to the type plant.

Deutzia

DEUTZIA

THIS IS A FAIRLY LARGE GENUS of shrubs, mainly from the Far East, to which a number of garden-bred hybrids and cultivars have been added. Their shape varies between those with elegant arching branches to those with a more stiff, erect, stance. The larger forms will reach up to 3m (10ft) or more. Their value lies in the profusion of pink or white flowers borne in the late spring or summer. These flowers have an open bell shape and appear in large clusters on the tips of the stems. Some of the more delightful forms are double. They are very hardy, though some of the early-flowering varieties can have the flower buds spoilt by late frosts.

Deutzia kalmiiflora

There is no problem with soils as they will tolerate most types, but the soil should be moisture retentive and should not be allowed to dry out. Deutzia can be sited in either full sun or light shade, although the former produces a better show of flowers.

This is a delightful shrub that can easily be placed in a variety of situations. In the shrubbery, deutzias look happy with the darker colours of weigelas or abelias, but they are equally attractive in the herbaceous or mixed border, particularly in soft schemes with other pinks or blues. Try, for example, growing forget-me-nots around the base of a deutzia. The white deutzias are useful for cooling down hotter colours.

Deutzias can be propagated readily from cuttings taken in summer, or from hardwood cuttings taken later in the year. Pruning should be carried out after flowering, when some of the old wood should be removed, encouraging new flowering shoots.

Deutzia chunii is a delightful shrub with arching stems bearing long bunches of white flowers opening from pink buds in summer.

D. × *elegantissima* is a more erect plant with rose-pink flowers. Darker pink flowers are found in the forms 'FASCICULATA' and 'ROSEALIND', the latter being the most commonly available.

D. gracilis, Slender Deutzia, offers pure white flowers in late spring. This is a smaller bush and is sometimes forced, so it could be used in tubs in a conservatory for a good spring effect.

D. × *hybrida* is a collection of hybrids of different colours, of which 'MONT ROSE', with its deep rose-pink flowers, flecked with a deeper colour, is one of the best.

D. × *kalmiiflora* has more open flowers with a deep pink colour outside and white inside. This is a smaller shrub than the other.

D. × *magnifica* is an erect shrub with delightful white double flowers.

D. × *rosea* is basically a pink hybrid but it has a number of forms of different shades. These include the popular 'CARMINEA', which has carmine-red flowers on a small (1m; 3ft) but spreading shrub.

D. scabra is mainly available in some of its several forms. 'CANDIDISSIMA' has pure white, double flowers. 'FLORE PLENO' is another double form; this time a pale purple on the outer petals and white on the inner ones.

There are many other forms to choose from but they are mainly variations on the same theme of shades of pink and height and shape of the shrub.

Deutzia × *magnifica*

Embothrium

Dorycnium hirsutum

Dorycnium

DORYCNIUM

THIS IS A SMALL SHRUB that deserves to be better known. It has small leaflets covered in hairs. These complement the small white or pink-flushed flowers. These are pea-like and appear, several to a terminal head, in summer. The flowers are followed by short cylindrical pods that are a shiny, red-brown colour. All these elements mix together to give a very satisfying bush only 60cm (2ft) tall. It is fairly hardy down to −8 or −10°C (17° or 14°F).

As long as it is well drained, any soil will suit dorycnium, but it should be in full sun.

This plant fits in happily with many arrangements as long as it is towards the front of the border. It goes well into silver borders, or those with soft colours. But it will equally well mix happily with stronger colours. I have it growing with a dark purple marjoram, but it would also make a pleasant blend with one of the sedums that has dark purple leaves. It can be used for cooling hot colours.

There are several species in this genus, but the one in cultivation and described above is *Dorycnium hirsutum*.

Embothrium

CHILEAN FIRE BUSH

ONE OF THE MOST exotic flowering shrubs for the garden, the Chilean fire bush, is covered with a mass of tubular, orange-scarlet flowers, creating the illusion that the whole shrub is nothing but a ball of fire. Far-fetched, perhaps, but it is a sight worth seeing during the late spring or early summer. There are only a few members of the genus and only one, *E. coccineum*, is in cultivation, though it has several forms. It grows quite tall, 6m (20ft) eventually, but takes quite a few years to reach its full height. It is on the tender side of hardy (−10°C; 14°F) and you should give it some protection, such as a wall, to be certain that it will survive the winter − this is not the kind of plant you want to lose.

A lime-free soil is necessary, preferably a rich, moisture-retentive one. The Chilean fire bush likes the sun and hates being over-crowded with other plants. In colder areas it might be safer to plant it in a conservatory.

Such a spectacular plant as this is a centre of attention and should be treated as such. Its need for wall protection in some parts may limit its positioning, but it looks fine on its own or backed by taller green trees or shrubs.

This shrub can be propagated from seed or from layers taken from the lower branches.

Embothrium coccineum

Pruning is restricted to keeping the bush tidy: it can be cut back, but will take a while to regenerate.

The species, *Embothrium coccineum*, is widely available, as are some of its forms, particularly *E.c. lanceolatum*, which has bright scarlet flowers and is usually considered more hardy than the type-plant. 'LONGIFOLIUM' is hardier still and is distinguished by its narrow leaves and vigorous growth.

Erica

HEATH

BEING SMALL, HEATHS ARE not always thought of as shrubs, but a closer look at their stems will reveal that they are decidedly woody. In any case, not all heaths are small; the so-called tree heaths are taller and more obviously shrubs (in spite of their name). The flowers are generally bell-shaped, and held either in whorls at the end of the branches, or, more commonly, singly along the whole length of the branch. The colour varies from white to a whole range from pink to deep red or purple. The leaves are very fine and needle-like, and again the colour range is extensive, from soft grey greens to dark green and golden yellow. Another aspect of their versatility is that they

Erica cinerea 'ATRORUBENS'

Erica

Zone 6

offer a range of plants that will give continual flowering throughout the year. With the exception of the tree heaths they are all hardy and will stand most weather.

Ericas are notorious lime haters, but fortunately there are two exceptions, *E. herbacea* (formerly *E. carnea*) and *E. terminalis*, that will grow even on chalk and have a good range of colours. All types will take sun or light de, but the deeper the shade, the more leggy the plants and the shyer they become of flowering.

Where do you put heaths? This is more of a problem than it seems. They certainly look out of place in an herbaceous border, but they just manage to look right on the margins of a shrubbery. They probably look best in a border of their own, along with a few small broadleaf shrubs such as rhododendron. There has been a tendency in recent years to have vast heather beds with conifers dotted around like tombstones. This, I feel, shows a lack of imagination. No matter how well you try to mix the colours and the shapes it still turns out deadly dull.

Heaths make good ground cover and can be used as fillers between shrubs that still have

Erica herbacea 'SPRINGWOOD WHITE'

some way to grow. The winter-flowering clones are worth siting where they can be seen without leaving paths or for brightening up corners that can be seen from the house during the bleak months. Most bear brown seed cases that can be an added bonus but you must keep this in mind when making a colour plan – they can always be sheared off.

Erica can be propagated by taking cuttings in summer or by layering plants. The latter can be achieved by burying a young plant some 5 or 7cm (2 or 3in) below its normal level in moist peat. When roots have formed on each stem they can be detached and potted up. Pruning is restricted to shearing over after flowering to keep the plants compact.

There are several hundred different forms available from nurseries and garden centres and it is impossible to describe more than just a few to show the range available.

Erica arborea, Tree Heath, is the odd one out in that it forms a substantial shrub. In favourable areas, in fact, it will grow up to 6m (20ft), though normally it will not reach this height. The flowers are easily recognizable as heath. They are usually white and have the added bonus of being scented. *E. australis* is a much smaller tree heath, with pink flowers. Unfortunately it is not so hardy.

E. ciliaris, Dorset Heath, has whorls of pink flowers at the ends of its branches. These

Erica arborea 'CONTORTA'

flowers are more inflated than those of some of the other heaths. The leaves are a soft grey green. There are quite a number of forms available, the two most popular being 'CORFE CASTLE', a rich pink, and 'STOBOROUGH', which is a pure white. They flower from midsummer to the end of autumn.

Erica cinerea, Bell Heather, has even more inflated corollas than the previous plant. These are available in a range of rich pinks and purples as well as white. This is a summer to early autumn flowering species, and there are over 100 varieties from which to choose. They include a few with foliage of a different colour than the normal grey green; 'GOLDEN DROP', for example, has copper-gold leaves.

E. × *darleyensis* has narrower flowers, appearing during the spring. It has the complete range of heath colours and, as with the other species mentioned, there are many named cultivars from which to choose.

E. erigena, Mediterranean Heath, has narrow flowers that appear during the winter and early spring. These are fragrant, and the various clones cover a range of colours from deep pink to white.

E. herbacea (still sometimes called *E. carnea*) is valuable because it will grow in limy conditions, even on chalk, though it is equally useful in other conditions as it flowers during the winter and early spring. There are very

Erica cinerea 'CEVENNES'

many forms, including some with foliage variations, such as yellow leaves.

E. tetralix, Cross-leaved Heath, is distinguished by having its small leaves arranged in fours, in the shape of a cross, up the stem. It flowers in summer and early autumn and offers a good range of colours.

E. vagans, Cornish Heath, has very small flowers that hang on the plant from summer to early autumn. Many forms are available, offering a good range of colours, including golden foliage in some varieties.

Escallonia

ESCALLONIA

THIS IS A POPULAR fast-growing shrub, reaching up to 3m (10ft) at maturity, and is suitable for the smaller garden. The flowers are bell shaped and the colours vary from white, through differing shades of pink, to red. They appear in late spring and early summer. Most species are evergreen with quite small, glossy green leaves.

Escallonia soon forms a large airy bush, with long arching stems, but it is quite easy to control in the smaller garden. It can be used in groupings or as a specimen shrub at the back of an herbaceous border. The various shades of red and pink allow it to fit into a red or purple planting scheme and the bright glossy foliage makes it a perfect foil for bright-coloured plants. Escallonias also make a dense, informal hedge that again can be used as a background – for example, behind an herbaceous border – and they make very good windbreaks near the sea.

This is a shrub that will take most soils except the most alkaline. It is fairly hardy (−10°C; 14°F).

Escallonias can easily be propagated from cuttings taken in late summer. Pruning should be restricted to removing some of the old wood immediately after flowering. If they are to be used as hedges they should not be regularly clipped, unless flowers are not required, as they appear on the old wood of the previous year's growth.

The South American genus *Escallonia* consists of about 60 species, but few of these are in cultivation, and in gardens the genus is mainly represented by a number of named varieties. Most important among these are the following colour forms, many of which were originated by the Donard Nursery: 'DONARD WHITE' and 'IVEYI' (both white); 'APPLE BLOSSOM', 'DONARD GEM', 'DONARD SEEDLING', 'GWENDOLYN ANLEY' and 'PEACH BLOSSOM' (all pale pink); 'DONARD RADIANCE', 'DONARD STAR', 'EDINENSIS' and 'INGRAMII' (all darker pink), and 'C.F. BALL', 'COMPACTA', 'DONARD BEAUTY', 'DONARD BRILLIANCE', 'LANGLEY-ENSIS' and 'WOODSIDE' (red).

Of the species that are available, *E. bifida* is by far the best, loved by bees and butterflies as well as humans. It has masses of white flowers that appear in the autumn and like most of the species it is on the tender side, appreciating the warmth of a wall. Another tender species is *E. macrantha*, this time with red, scented flowers that appear earlier than those of *E. bifida*.

Escallonia

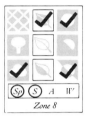

Zone 8

Escallonia 'SLIEVE DONARD'

Eucalyptus

Sp (S) (A) W

Zone 10

Eucalyptus

EUCALYPTUS, GUM TREE

IN GARDENING TERMS, one of Australia's greatest exports has been its gum trees. Although coming from a warm country, they can be seen in all parts of the globe, including those that have quite severe winters. In cooler regions they are known mainly for their foliage and bark, but there are many beautiful flowering species that can be grown. Many gum trees will reach great heights and are only suitable for the largest gardens. If cut hard back, many will shoot again from the base, thus keeping small and compact, but this is usually at the expense of the flowers. Like the flowers of so many Australian trees and shrubs, the beauty of a gum tree flower is derived from its boss of coloured stamens. The leaves of the many species (over 500) come in various shapes, but all have a distinct juvenile phase which is different from their mature shape. Many species are relatively hardy in colder countries, though they may be cut back by severe frosts and by freezing winds. Unfortunately the more spectacular flowerers are among the more tender species.

Eucalyptus seem to tolerate a wide range of soils, and will survive in quite dry conditions. They normally grow in full sun.

Eucalyptus rhodantha

Eucalyptus macrocarpa

The fine flowering forms of these trees are grown as specimen plants: they are far too large and spectacular to be part of a border.

Propagation is from seed, which takes at least a year to ripen. Pruning is not necessary. Trees are often pollarded to maintain a supply of juvenile foliage, but this will reduce the number of flowers and may prevent the tree from flowering at all.

Eucalyptus caesia, is a small, well-shaped tree, up to 6m (20ft) high, with pink flowers set off by the tree's general powdery grey appearance.

E. calophylla, Marri, is a tree of variable height, with flowers formed of white, pale yellow or pale pink stamens.

E. eximia, Yellow Bloodwood, has both yellow flowers and a yellowish bark. It is a medium-sized tree.

E. ficifolia, the Red-flowering Gum, forms a small tree, up to 9m (30ft) high, and is covered in masses of scarlet-red flowers from the late summer on. The evergreen foliage is broadly lanceolate in its adult form.

E. macrocarpa, Bluebush, is a silver-leaved shrub of somewhat loose habit that is covered with large flowers of red stamens and yellow anthers.

E. phoenicia, Scarlet Gum, has very attractive scarlet flowers on a medium-sized tree.

E. pyriformis, Pear-fruited Mallee, is another of the red-flowered eucalyptus. This one is a large shrub, its name being derived from its large pear-shaped fruit.

E. × *rhodantha*, Rose Mallee, is a loose shrub growing up to about 3m (10ft). The flowers are large balls of red stamens, studded with gold-tipped anthers, and are produced in profusion.

E. torquata, Coral Gum, a tree reaching about 7m (23ft) in height is another red-flowered species.

Eucryphia

EUCRYPHIA

Eucryphia glutinosa

Eucryphia

Sp (*S*) (*A*) *W*

Zone 8

EUCRYPHIAS ARE AN OUTSTANDING small group of free-flowering trees that are much neglected. The cause of this neglect is difficult to see as the trees are easy to propagate and require no special attention, yet they are smothered in beautiful white flowers in late summer and autumn when few other trees are in bloom. The flowers are up to 5cm (2in) in diameter, saucer-shaped and with a pronounced tuft of stamens. Most eucryphias are

Eucryphia × *nymanensis* 'NYMANSAY'

evergreen but they can burn in strong cold winds. They eventually reach a tree size of up to 11m (35ft), but because they are slow growing they are often seen as shrubs. Fortunately, they start flowering at an early age, even when they are only a couple of feet high, so they earn their keep right from the start. They form an upright, often columnar shape, and are moderately hardy, taking temperatures down to −12°C (10°F).

Eucryphias are not too selective about the soil in which they grow but they prefer a cool, moist root run and the soil should not be too alkaline. Plenty of light is essential for good flowering but full sun should be avoided unless the lower part of the tree is shaded so that the roots are cool.

The tall columnar shape filled with glistening white flowers would make this an ideal specimen tree at some focal point in the garden except for the fact that its leaves are a bit dull for the greater part of the year. It can still be treated as a specimen, but it is probably best planted against a background of other trees, and with shrubs round its feet, rather than standing alone in a prominent position.

No pruning is required, and propagation is easily achieved from semi-ripe cuttings taken in late summer.

Eucryphias originate from Australia and Chile, and quite a number of species and hybrids are available. *E. cordifolia* is more tolerant of chalky soils than the others but is not quite so hardy. *E. glutinosa* is hardier and has larger flowers. Unlike the others it is deciduous and not so easy to propagate. *E. ×* *intermedia* 'ROSTREVOR' and *E. × nymanensis* 'NYMANSAY' are two popular hybrids, the former being fragrant. The Tasmanian *E. lucida* is likewise fragrant. Closely allied is another Tasmanian, *E. milliganii*, which is not so tall and has smaller flowers.

Euphorbia splendens milli

Euphorbia

Zone 10

Euphorbia

EUPHORBIA, SPURGE

THIS IS A MOST EXTRAORDINARY genus. Some are only centimetres high and grow as weeds; some are viciously spined and look like cacti; some are herbaceous and grace our gardens with a cool lush greenness; some grow as tough gnarled desert trees, while others sport coloured bracts and serve us as garden shrubs or potted plants. Lucky would be the man who could have a garden that encompassed all these variations, which are spread over more than 1000 species. Euphorbias are so diverse that it is difficult to give a generalized description. One feature that they all have in common is a milky substance that oozes from cut stems. This can cause irritation to sensitive skins, and should certainly be kept away from eyes. (The flow of sap can be staunched with a lighted match or by dipping the cut stem in fine sand.) While most of the herbaceous plants are hardy, their shrubby brethren are decidedly tender and can only be grown in frost-free areas. In colder regions, they can be

Euphorbia pulcherrima (red form)

Euphorbia fulgens

Euphorbia pulcherrima (pink form)

grown in a warm greenhouse.

They all appreciate well-drained soil and plenty of sun. They are mainly propagated by hardwood cuttings.

Euphorbia fulgens, Scarlet Plume, is an evergreen shrub, up to 1.5m (5ft) tall. The colourful feature is the floral bracts that surround the flower in winter; these are bright scarlet. Scarlet Plume is tender and should be protected from frosts.

E. leucocephala, White Lace Bush, is another evergreen shrub, in this case covered in white flowers during the winter months. It flowers best in hot climates.

E. milii, Crown of Thorns, is a spiny stemmed plant. It has a few small green leaves and clusters of small red bracts. It is suitable for rock gardens in warmer areas or for use as a house plant in cooler ones. It grows to about a metre (3ft).

E. pulcherrima, Poinsettia, is the most famous of the shrubby spurges. It is widely grown outside in hotter climates and used as a house plant in colder ones. It is characterized by the brilliant red bracts that surround the yellow flowers throughout the winter. There are now many good strains available, particularly the double, 'HENRIETTE ECKE', and those of the Hegg strain.

Forsythia

FORSYTHIA

ANY OBJECTION TO FORSYTHIA is not to the myriads of gold stars that it produces in spring, but to the rather soulless plant that remains for the rest of the year. The flowers are in the shape of flared bells and are usually a rich golden yellow. They are borne before or just as the leaves are appearing in the early spring. Forsythia is very hardy and has no problems with the weather. It grows up to 4m (13ft) high.

It is not at all fussy about soils – it will take almost any type – nor is it worried about location, although it prefers full sun if it is to flower at its best.

The strident yellow is acceptable on its own but it may clash with other shades, sometimes even with daffodils. It looks striking against a blue sky, if you can find one, or lacking that, against the green of other shrubs. It is best tucked away at the back of a border, where it can be appreciated in spring but covered up by later flowers in summer. It can also be used as a hedge.

Propagation is easy, either from summer cuttings or from layering those with arching stems. Pruning should be carried out after flowering when some of the old wood should be completely removed. Forsythia can be cut

Forsythia 'ARNOLD GIANT'

Forsythia

Sp S A W
Zone 7

Forsythia × intermedia 'SPECTABILIS'

Fremontodendron

Zone 7

Fremontodendron

FREMONTIA

THIS IS A VERY small genus of shrubs, of which only one, *F. californicum*, is in general cultivation. The flowers are a most glorious golden yellow and 7.5-10cm (2-3in) across. They appear from late spring right through to autumn. Although it need not worry anybody, this plant, in spite of its appearance, has no petals; it is the calyx or sepals that are yellow. This is a fine botanical distinction that may be of interest to some people but should make no difference to the appreciation of the plant. What might make a difference is the retention of the calyces after the flower is over – they turn brown and shrivel, though with time and patience they can be removed. The leaves are actually leaves and look like leaves, with a heart shape and a soft downy underside. Fremontodendrons are evergreen or semi-evergreen. They can be grown as free-standing trees but it is more usual to grow them as wall shrubs, where they will make up to 6m

Fremontodendron californicum 'CALIFORNIA GLORY'

to the ground but will take a couple of seasons to recover.

Forsythia 'ARNOLD DWARF' has a compact stature, but not very much to offer in the flowering line. 'ARNOLD GIANT', on the other hand, has large flowers and vigorous growth.

There are several forms of *F. × intermedia* available, but three in particular are popular: 'LYNWOOD', which is a very good flowering form, 'SPRING GLORY', a free-flowering variety, and 'SPECTABILIS', with its golden yellow flowers.

F. ovata 'TETRAGOLD' has large flowers that arrive earlier than many of the other varieties.

F. suspensa has several good forms that are borne on long arching branches.

F. viridissima, usually seen in its form 'BROXENSIS', has pale flowers.

Having done my duty and described them, I am still not certain that I like forsythias. The one good point is that branches can be cut in winter and brought inside where they soon open their flowers and leaves, long before these appear outside.

Fuchsia

Zone 8-9

FUCHSIA

EVERYONE KNOWS AND LOVES these plants and I tend to go along with the crowd, but I must admit that when displayed in serried ranks at a flower show they can look overpowering. These are delightful as single plants or in groups of the same type, but mix them higgledy-piggledy and you need to reach for your sunglasses. The flowers themselves come in a range of pinks, reds, mauves, purples and white, separately or in combinations. Strangely, this is the second plant in a row where the calyx and sepals play an important part. In the fuchsia, the calyx and sepals are generally red, with the four sepals standing out like a ballerina's skirt. The petals are folded or pleated like an inner skirt, through which the stamens hang. The whole flower hangs down from the branches, giving rise to mental images ranging from dancers to earrings. Fuchsias will flower throughout the warmer months, from late spring up to

Fremontodendron californicum 'CALIFORNIA GLORY'

(20ft) in growth. Although they are reputed to be tender, I have known a specimen up against a south wall that has come through two winters at temperatures down to −17°C (1°F).

Fremontodendrons will tolerate most types of soil and although they will put up with a little shade, they prefer full sun.

This is a magnificent plant and well worth a place on a sunny wall. Since it flowers for most of the warmer part of the year, its neighbours must be chosen with care – the blues of a ceanothus or *Solanum crispum* would look well.

Propagation takes place from seed or from cuttings in summer. No pruning is required except what is necessary to keep the shrub tidy and within bounds.

There are a couple of cultivars available: 'CALIFORNIA GLORY' and 'PACIFIC SUNSET', both with larger flowers than the type-plant. Occasionally one might come across *Fremontodendron mexicanum* which is more tender than *F. californicum*. Its flowers are darker in colour than those of *F. californicum* and have narrower sepals, giving it a spikier appearance.

Fuchsia magellanica

autumn frosts. The bushes vary in height and compactness but many have graceful, arching stems, liberally hung with these bright flowers. The leaves, on the whole, are quite small, and there are various shades of green as well as some pleasant variegated forms. Fuchsias can be left outside permanently, treated as bedding plants, or overwintered in tubs or pots and brought outside in spring. If left outside during the winter, they are liable to get cut back by frosts, and in severe weather the rootstock may be killed. To help to prevent this they should be planted deeply and, in colder areas, given an extra mulch.

There is no problem with the type of soil as long as it is reasonably well drained. Fuchsias prefer sun, but will certainly take a bit of light shade.

These are marvellous plants for either a shrubbery or a mixed border. Their tendency to be cut down each winter gives them a natural affinity with the herbaceous border, while their colour and size make them appropriate in any colour scheme, except perhaps a yellow one. They look particularly good with blues and bronzy purples. They can be grown in pots or hanging baskets in a cool, moist conservatory.

Fuchsias are propagated from summer cuttings. Plants that have received a winter frosting should be pruned back to ground

Fuchsia 'LENA'

level in spring. Those that come through the winter can be left unpruned except for the removal of some of the old wood and a general tidying up of the plant.

There are thousands of fuchsias to choose from and there is no doubt that the choice is a very subjective one. I would strongly suggest that the reader should look at trade stands at shows, or look round nurseries. If possible, try to isolate the plant at which you are looking from its surrounding distractions, a visual trick that is by no means easy. Fortunately there are plenty of easily-grown fuchsias from which to choose, so check that it is not one you have to cosset; if it is, then there are plenty of other options. The following are a few of the more popular.

Fuchsia fulgens has very long pendulous flowers. These are vermilion and appear in clusters at the end of the branches. This fuchsia has larger leaves than most other species. There are several varieties of which *F.f.* var *gesneriana* has laxer growth and shorter flowers than the species. *F.f.* var *rubra grandiflora* is generally supposed to be the best form.

F. 'LADY THUMB' is a new relative of 'TOM THUMB' (see below) and both have the same qualities – very small flowers, free flowering habit and compactness. 'LADY THUMB' is semi-double with white petals.

F. 'LENA' is semi-double with a flesh pink

Fuchsia 'MRS POPPLE'

top, slightly reflexed, and a rose-magenta skirt. It is a fine old cultivar that has been valued for its ability to be trained to any shape.

F. magellanica is a very popular species, with several well-known forms. It is the hardiest of the fuchsias. The flowers are quite small but it is free flowering with a red top and a purple lower half. *F.m. gracilis* 'VARIEGATA' has silver-variegated foliage. *F.m.* 'RICCARTONII' is possibly the most vigorous of the hardy fuchsias. After being cut back in winter it will grow from 1.5 to 2m (5 to 6ft) in one season. It is particularly good for hedges. The flowers are quite small with scarlet sepals and a dark purple corolla. *F.m.* 'VERSICOLOR' has extremely attractive silver-grey foliage with pink and creamy white variegations.

F. 'MRS POPPLE' is one of the largest of the hardy varieties. It is an old and popular cultivar with a scarlet top and a rich purple-violet skirt.

F. 'TOM THUMB' has very small flowers that appear in profusion. They are carmine and mauve. The plant itself is attractive and compact, growing up to 50cm (1.5ft).

Gardenia

GARDENIA

AS A GARDEN SHRUB, the gardenia takes a lot of beating, with its scented flowers and its glossy evergreen leaves. Although the most popular species have white flowers there are several other colours, including yellow and pink. They make cool elegant flowers for cutting, particularly the double forms, which perfume the whole room. As one would expect from a large genus of over 200 species, there is quite a variation in height, from small shrubs to modest trees, but those in cultivation do not normally exceed 3m (10ft). Their big drawback is that they are decidedly tender: they will not tolerate frost and prefer a warm climate if they are to perform at their best. In colder areas, it is perfectly possible to grow them under glass as long as a reasonable temperature (16°C; 60°F) is maintained.

Gardenia jasminoides

Another, but minor, drawback is that some species are armed with spines.

Gardenias are not too fussy over soil, though they prefer it to be moderately acid. They should have a free-draining soil but should be kept well-watered throughout the growing period, with less water during the winter months. The best position is in partial shade, away from the full force of the sun.

Gardenias can be used as border plants or

Gardenia thunbergia

Gardenia

Sp (S) A W

Zone 10

as specimens, placed where the full glory of the flowers and their scent can be appreciated: near an open window would be a good position, for example. They make ideal conservatory plants as long as the temperature can be maintained during the winter months.

Gardenias can be propagated either from seed or from hardwood cuttings, preferably in the early winter. No pruning is required.

Gardenia jasminoides (G. angusta) is a medium-sized shrub of up to 2m (6ft) high, with white shallow flowers. It has no spines. There are several very good forms, including 'GRANDIFLORA', 'FLORIDA', 'FORTUNEANA' and 'VEITCHIANA' (winter flowering), which have larger flowers, some of them double or semi-double. 'PROSTRATA' and 'RADICANS' are both low-growing forms.

G. spathulifolia is a small tree, up to 5m (17ft) high, with creamy white flowers that yellow as they age.

G. thunbergia is intermediate between the last two, growing up to 3m (10ft). It has the typical, shallow dish-shaped flowers, glistening white in colour and perfumed.

Garrya elliptica

Garrya

TASSEL BUSH

FORTUNATELY, WHEN THE TASSEL BUSH was created it was decided to let it flower in winter; in summer it would have been so drab that it would have gone unnoticed. It is surprising how many people do not see it even in winter, often walking straight past, but when they have had their attention drawn to it, they exclaim in delight. In the middle of winter, when little else is around, this subtle bush has grey-green chains of flowers, hanging from among glossy green foliage. It has a further advantage in that it is not averse to a bit of shade and can therefore be placed on the north side of a building. It is hardy, taking temperatures down to at least −15°C (5°F), but although it grows perfectly well as a free-standing shrub, it is often grown against a wall. It grows up to 4m (13ft).

The tassel bush is quite happy with both acid and alkaline soils. Similarly, it tolerates both sun or partial shade.

There is no problem with positioning as far as winter is concerned, as there is little with which to associate it, but since it has not got much to offer in the summer the tassel bush should be tucked away, hence the north wall. It can look leaden here, though, and it is a good idea to put something with it that will brighten the shade a bit. A light-coloured clematis, that will be cut back in the winter, might be sited to grow through it.

Propagation is from summer cuttings. No pruning is required other than keeping the shrub trim.

Garrya elliptica is the only genus widely available from most garden centres and nurseries. It has a cultivar, 'JAMES ROOF', that is also common. This has longer and thicker tassels than the species.

Garrya

| Sp | S | A | W |

Zone 7

Gaultheria shallon

Gaultheria

GAULTHERIA

THIS IS A VERY LARGE GENUS of dwarf shrubs, and those that are in cultivation make excellent ground cover. The flowers are in the shape of urns or bells, like lilies-of-the-valley. They are usually white, though there are some pink forms, and they appear in late spring or early summer. Following the flowers, attractive round fruits appear, and these also come in a variety of colours, including pink, red, purple, blue and white. The leaves are evergreen and vary in shape from ovate to narrow, almost like short yew leaves. Gaultherias rarely grow above 60cm (2ft) and most are much smaller. On the whole they are pretty hardy, taking temperatures down to −15°C (5°F).

Once again we have a member of the heather family, the Ericaceae, and it does not like limy soils in any form. It does not mind shade, but flowers better in full sun, though it is essential that it has moisture at its roots.

These plants offer attractive and interesting ground cover, especially when associated with other lovers of acid soils, such as rhododendrons, camellias or pieris. Some can be invasive, so do not plant these close to choice plants in an herbaceous border.

Propagation can take place from seed or semi-ripe cuttings. Most species spread by underground stems; these can be broken and the plant divided. Pruning is restricted to keeping the plants tidy, though they can be cut to the ground if necessary.

Gaultheria cuneata is a good compact form, only growing a few centimetres above the ground. It has lovely glossy leaves, tinted with red in the winter, white flowers and white fruit.

G. procumbens, Creeping Wintergreen, is the most commonly available. This has white flowers and red fruit on a good compact shape. The leaves take on a reddish tinge in winter.

G. shallon comes next in the popularity stakes. This has flowers that are tinged with pink, and purple fruit.

Several more species and cultivars are available, but these have to be searched for in the specialist nurseries.

Gaultheria cuneata

Gaultheria

Sp S A W
Zone 7

Genista aetnensis

Genista

Zone 8

Genista

BROOM

THIS IS ANOTHER FAMILY of brooms (*Cytisus* and *Spartium* being the others). This one restricts itself to variations on yellow. The flowers are pea-like in shape and absolutely smother the branches in spring or summer. It is impossible to imagine a more solid block of yellow in the garden. As with the other brooms, the green stems do not produce many leaves and those that do appear are small and usually lanceolate in shape. Genista are reasonable hardy, taking temperatures down to −15°C (5°F). Most form quite compact bushes, only growing to between 1 and 1.25m (3 and 4 ft).

There are no problems over soil types. They prefer sun but will tolerate a bit of light shade, though with the usual proviso that they will not flower as well in shade.

These are marvellous for brightening up a dull corner or a solid mass of green foliage. Some of the small forms can be used in rockeries and look particularly good tumbling down a wall or bank.

Genista can be propagated from softwood cuttings in summer. No pruning is required.

Genista aetnensis, Mount Etna Broom, is the exception as far as height is concerned, growing up to 4m (13ft). It flowers in early summer when it has masses of golden yellow flowers on gracefully arching branches.

G. hispanica, Spanish Gorse, has lighter flowers and forms a rounded hummock. This one can be a bit vicious as it has spikes on its stems.

G. lydia is the one to plant on the wall or bank as it has a more prostrate habit and long arching branches. The flowers are a good golden yellow.

G. tinctoria, Dyer's Greenweed, has leaves

that are more numerous and narrower in shape than those of other species. The yellow flowers are borne throughout the summer. There are several forms available including 'FLORE PLENO' which has double flowers, giving it an intense yellow appearance.

Genista lydia

Grevillea

GREVILLEA

HAILING FROM AUSTRALIA, it is the quantity and diversity of these evergreen shrubs and trees that makes them so interesting. The colour range of the flowers is increasing all the time as new hybrids are introduced, with blue being the only colour missing. The flowers are curiously shaped tubes, out through which the style sticks like a tongue. The leaves vary a great deal in shape but are generally very attractive. Height varies from prostrate plants to giant trees. Hardiness is debatable. Generally it is assumed that Grevilleas are tender and will not tolerate much frost, but it is worth experimenting as some may be hardier than is generally thought.

They will thrive in any well drained soil and should be provided with a sunny position.

Grevilleas are very versatile as garden plants and can be used in a variety of positions either in a border or as specimen shrubs. The diversity of colour gives them a wide range of associating plants. The low-growing ones make good ground cover and can be used effectively between other trees and shrubs. In colder areas the smaller shrubs can make ideal pot plants for warm conservatories and greenhouses.

Propagation is from seed, but some of the newer cultivars and hybrids are better taken from semi-ripe or hardwood cuttings. No pruning is necessary except in the case of some of the shrubby ones to keep them tidy. This should be carried out after flowering.

Grevillea alpina is a shrub growing up to 2m (6ft) tall though often shorter. The flower colour varies, but is basically red at the base and yellowish at the top. It is one of the hardiest. 'DALLACHIANA' is a popular cultivar with red and cream flowers.

G. biternata is very low growing and makes excellent ground cover. Its flowers are creamy coloured and sweetly scented.

G. caleyi is a long flowering shrub of up to 3m (10ft) with flowers of deep rose to red. It has deeply divided leaves.

G. juniperina has juniper-shaped leaves and various coloured flowers, mainly red. The several cultivars include 'MOLONGLO', 'RUBRA' and 'TRINERVA', which is low growing.

G. rosmarinifolia is a popular dense shrub

Grevillea

Sp (*S*) (*A*) *W*
Zone 10

Grevillea juniperina

Grevillea rosmarinifolia 'SPLENDENS'

of up to 2.5m (7ft). As the name suggests the leaves are narrow like rosemary's. The flowers are variable but basically crimson with pink and cream at the mouth of the tube. There are several cultivars including 'JENKINSII' with deep red flowers, and the creamy-yellow 'LUTEA'. *G. sericea* is a compact species of up to 2m (6ft) with rose coloured flowers.

G. sulphurea makes a dense bush of up to 2m (6ft) with pale yellow flowers. It is one of the hardiest and will take a few degrees of frost.

There are many modern hybrids, including 'CANBERRA GEM' (rich red); 'CROSBIE MORRISON' (dark red); 'GLEN SANDRA' (bright red); 'IVANHOE' (carmine red); 'OLYMPIC FLAME' (rosy red); and the 'POORINDA' cultivars which consist of many colour forms.

green as they are covered with a white, furry down. Halimiums grow to about a metre (3ft) in height. They are not very hardy, but will take frosts down to −5 or −8°C (23 or 18°F) if they have a certain amount of protection.

They will tolerate any soil but it must be free draining. Full sun is required.

These plants have a soft quality, making them very suitable for mixing with other such plants in a sunny border. They look particularly good against ceanothus.

Propagation is from seed or cuttings taken in summer. No pruning is required except to remove dead wood and generally keep the plant tidy.

Halimium lasianthum is the commonest

Halimium lasianthum

form available. It has grey-green leaves and yellow flowers with a brown blotch at the base of the petals. There is a variety called 'CONCOLOR' in which the blotch is absent.

Halimium

HALIMIUM

THIS IS A NICE little genus of plants that is not very well known. They are related to the rock roses (*Cistus*) which they closely resemble, except in one respect – they have yellow flowers. At the base of each petal is a dark purple or brown blotch. Each flower only lasts a day, but there is a succession of new buds throughout the summer. The leaves are a soft

Hamamelis

WITCH HAZEL

THIS MUST BE ONE of the finest of all the winter-flowering trees and shrubs. It bears knots of thin yellow ribbons, tied round the naked branches. There is now a wide range of varieties, and each year brings more, all variations on the yellow or orange theme. The

Halimium

Sp (*S*) *A W*
Zone 9

Hamamelis mollis

Hamamelis

Zone 6

soils, preferring neutral to acidic. It prefers full sun but will tolerate light shade.

A well-grown hamamelis is a magnificent sight in winter and care should be taken to make the most of this. It looks particularly striking when lit up by the winter sun and an attractive idea is to plant the small blue *Iris histrioides* around its skirts.

Hamamelis are propagated by grafting onto seedling stock of *H. virginiana*; a tedious business. With a great deal of patience they can also be layered. There are no short cuts and either method is a lengthy operation. Pruning is usually restricted to cutting material for the house, but do not be too lavish as hamamelis can be slow to break from old wood.

Hamamelis × intermedia has several forms, of which 'DIANE' is possibly the best, with rich, almost red coloration. 'JELENA' is another very good form with yellow-orange, almost brown flowers. 'MOONLIGHT' is a pale yellow.

H. mollis, Chinese Witch Hazel, are the best plants to go for. Although the other colours are intriguing and I like to see them, yellow is really the colour for this plant and that is what you get with *H. mollis*. In addition there is also that wonderful scent. There are some colour variations: 'PALLIDA' is a pale yellow and 'GOLDCREST' is a rich golden colour with a hint of red.

H. vernalis is a suckering, but quite small, bush. It is mainly seen in the form 'SANDRA', notable for its rich autumn colouring.

centre of the cluster of petals has a red glow. Some of the varieties have a fresh, almost astringent, smell. They are very good for cutting and bringing indoors. Early blooming forms tend to last longer, and forms that have shorter petals do not seem to die so quickly.

The leaves are ovate and hazel-like. They colour up quite well in the autumn. Hamamelis will eventually make quite a substantial shrub, up to 5m (16ft) high, and there is no problem with its hardiness, even when the flowers are fully out.

Hamamelis is a bit fussy with its choice of

Hamamelis × intermedia 'JELENA'

Hebe

SHRUBBY VERONICAS

THIS RICH GENUS OF hundreds of species and garden forms owes its existence to New Zealand, where hebes exist in the wild. Once suspected of being tender, it has been found that they are generally more hardy than was previously thought, and anyway can be easily overwintered as cuttings or as small plants that will quickly grow. There are basically two types: those with a pronounced flower

Hebe

Zone 7-10

Hebe salicifolia

spike – a bit like a test-tube brush for the chemically minded – and the whipcord hebes, which have very small leaves that are held close to the stem, giving the impression of cord. In the latter group it is the colour of the foliage rather than the flowers that is important, but the hebes with flower spikes are by far the majority. They are quick-growing shrubs that can even be treated as bedding plants and planted out from pots in the spring. The colours vary from white to blue, mauve, purple or red. Some spikes, usually those with larger, coarser, individual flowers, are lax, but those with smaller flowers are neat and compact. Those with the coarser flowers often also have larger leaves that are rather dull, both in individual and overall appearance. The size of the spikes can vary from almost nothing to 15cm (6in). The flowering season is long, from early summer to the end of autumn. The evergreen leaves also offer a

range of shapes and colours, and there are even variegated and silver-leaved varieties. Hardiness varies; an average could be given of −5°C (23°F), but individuals can survive down to −14°C (7°F). Height varies from prostrate to about 2m (6ft), but most are relatively small, making hebe an ideal plant for the small garden.

There are no problems with the soil type as long as it is free draining. Siting should be in full sun and away from frost hollows.

These are very decorative plants and can be used in a variety of positions, either as specimen plants or as part of a larger design. The softer colours would fit into a wide range of schemes, the silver-leaved varieties being especially valuable. Hebes are suitable for use as bedding plants or for growing in pots, if these can be given winter protection. The whipcords, with bronzy foliage, look highly attractive when positioned to catch the winter sunshine. They are salt tolerant and are suitable for seaside gardens.

Propagation is easily undertaken from summer cuttings. Pruning is restricted to trimming and occasionally (every four or five years) sacrificing a year's flowering by cutting back to promote new growth.

This is another one of those genera where it is best to go and see as many as you can and select those that suit your taste and

Hebe 'AUTUMN GLORY'

designs. Here are just a few of the hundreds available.

H. albicans is a dwarf grey-green shrub with white spikes of flowers.

H. armstrongii is one of the whipcord hebes. It has gold-green foliage. There is a dwarf form, *H.* 'JAMES STIRLING' that is suitable for the rock garden.

H. 'AUTUMN GLORY' is very popular, with masses of flowers over a long season. It has deep purple flowers and broad, dark green foliage.

H. 'CARL TESCHNER' is a very popular carpeting hebe. It has small leaves and small spikes of violet flowers.

H. macrantha has the largest flowers; these are pure white and are arranged in short spikes. Flowering starts in late spring.

H. 'MIDSUMMER BEAUTY' has very long lavender-purple flowers on a tall shrub with long leaves. The flowers are scented.

H. 'MRS WINDER' has good, blue-mauve flowers, but is often grown just for its superb bronze-purple leaves.

H. pinguifolia 'PAGEI' is a dwarf prostrate plant often grown on the rock garden as much for its silver foliage as for its spikes of white flowers. It is very hardy.

H. salicifolia is one of my favourites, with its willow-like leaves and an absolute profusion of long, pale mauve flower spikes that are

Hebe albicans

strongly scented. It forms a sizeable bush of up to 3m (10ft) high.

H. 'SIMON DELAUX' has very long flower spikes that are deep red in colour.

H. 'SPENCER'S SEEDLING' has very long racemes of white flowers and long narrow leaves.

Hebe 'MIDSUMMER BEAUTY'

Hedysarum

HEDYSARUM

AN ATTRACTIVE PLANT THAT is not seen very often, this has racemes of rose-purple, pea-like flowers held over pinnate, pale green leaves on arching stems. The whole bush has a light airy quality to it. Although this is quite a large genus in the wild, only *Hedysarum multijugum* is reasonably widely available from nurseries. It is quite a tall bush, reaching up to 3m (10ft), and is fairly hardy, tolerating frosts down to about −10°C (14°F), though it is advisable to plant it against a sunny wall in colder areas.

Hedysarum is very tolerant of all soil conditions as long as the earth is well drained. It prefers full sun.

This is a good shrub for borders based on shades of purple or blue. Elsewhere it might not prove too successful.

Hedysarum

Sp (S) (A) W

Zone 8

Hedysarum coronarium

Helianthemum nummularium

Propagation is from softwood cuttings in summer. Pruning is restricted to tidying up the bush and removing some of the old wood to encourage new growth.

Although *Hedysarum multijugum* is the main species, *H. coronarium*, which has fragrant, bright red flowers, is beginning to become available. Unfortunately, this last has the disadvantage of being short lived.

buds throughout the summer and autumn. These sprawling shrubs are not very tall (up to 30cm; 1ft) but have a girth two to three times greater than their height.

They are tolerant of any soil type including chalk, but prefer well-drained conditions. They are lovers of sun, as their name implies.

These are extremely useful plants. They make good fillers between other plants, particularly in an herbaceous or mixed border, where a rock rose makes an attractive link between two contrasting colours, parti-

Helianthemum nummularium 'WISLEY PRIMROSE'

Helianthemum

Sp (S) (A) W'
Zone 8

Helianthemum

ROCK ROSE; SUN ROSE

THESE ARE IMPORTANT PLANTS in any garden and sad is the design that manages without them. The mainly soft colours and grey foliage enable them to be used in a wide variety of positions. The flowers are small saucers of five petals, which only last a day. There are double forms and these retain their flowers a little longer, but in any case the daily loss is no problem as there is a continual renewal of

Helianthemum

cularly at the front of the border. Rock roses are perfect for rock gardens or for the top of a wall or bank, from where they can spill down. Likewise they can spill over the edges of paths to soften straight lines. They can also sprawl onto lawns, but will kill the grass that they cover.

Propagation can take place from summer cuttings or from seed. The latter is easy, but there is no control over the resulting colours. Pruning is restricted to cutting the plant back in the spring to prevent it becoming too leggy and to promote new growth.

There are over a hundred named forms from which to choose, most of these being varieties of *Helianthemum nummularium*, the only hardy species. Here are a few of the best: 'THE BRIDE' (creamy white with a yellow centre), 'CHERRY PINK' (deep pink), 'HENFIELD BRILLIANT' (deep orange), 'JUBILEE' (double, primrose yellow), 'MRS C.W. EARLE' (double, scarlet with yellow at the base), 'WISLEY PINK' (pale pink with orange centre), 'WISLEY PRIMROSE' (primrose yellow – a vigorous plant).

Hibiscus

ROSE OF SHARON; TREE HOLLYHOCK

THIS IS ONE OF the mallow family, the Malvaceae; a fact about which the flowers will leave you in no doubt. These are large flared trumpets in shape and have a gorgeous colour range of blues, pinks, reds, purples and white. They can be found as single, double or semi-double flowering plants. They are deciduous and the leaves are roughly ovate in shape, and mid-green in colour. This is a very effective, late-flowering shrub, reaching up to about 3m (6ft) in height.

The hibiscus is reasonably tolerant of frosts down to about −12 or −15°C (10 or 5°F), though there are some that will take no frost at all and these must obviously be confined to warmer areas or to the conservatory, for which they are admirably suited.

They will tolerate most soils as long as they are not too wet, and they are happy in sun or light shade.

Hibiscus flower in late summer into the autumn and can be used as specimen shrubs or mixed in with other plants in the shrubbery or herbaceous border. The colours and upright shape are very suitable for the latter, particularly in designs based on purple or blue. A hibiscus can also make a subtly

Hibiscus rosa-sinensis

Hibiscus

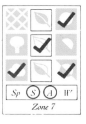

Sp S A W
Zone 7

Hibiscus syriacus 'BLUEBIRD'

Hibiscus syriacus 'RED HEART'

pleasing contrast in a silver border.

Propagation is from summer cuttings. Pruning is restricted to tidying the plant.

Hibiscus rosa-sinensis is tender and can only be grown outside in warm, frost-free areas, but it makes an excellent shrub for the conservatory or greenhouse. If grown in a tub it can be brought onto a sunny patio in summer.

H. syriacus is the species that is commonly seen in gardens. It has given rise to quite a number of cultivars. 'BLUEBIRD' is one of the most famous. This has violet-blue flowers

with a reddish centre. 'DIANA' has large white flowers, and 'DUC DU BRABANT' has deep crimson, double flowers. 'HAMABO' is popular, with pale pink flowers and a crimson eye. 'RED HEART' is white with a crimson centre, and 'WILLIAM E. SMITH' has pure white flowers with frilled edges. 'WOODBRIDGE' has large rosy-crimson flowers with a darker centre.

Hoheria

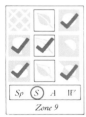

Hoheria

Sp (S) A W

Zone 9

Hibiscus rosa-sinensis

Hoheria

HOHERIA

ALTHOUGH IT IS NOT a very large country, New Zealand has added a tremendous amount of beauty to gardens all over the world. Unfortunately, New Zealand is not quite cold enough and many of the fine plants that have been introduced elsewhere prove to be on the tender side in their new setting. With smaller shrubs this is not too much of a problem, as they are easy to protect or even replace if necessary, but with trees and taller shrubs it is a different matter. *Hoheria* is one of those genera with beautiful flowers that make it well worth growing, but it is often ignored because it is on the tender side, taking frosts down to only −5°C (23°F) or so. It is definitely worth trying in warmer temperate areas against a sunny wall, possibly with a bit of added winter protection. The translucent pure white saucers are held in large clusters during the summer. To add to this, they are fragrant with the scent of honey.

Hoherias will grow in most soils, though they are not so keen on the more limy ones. They will tolerate full sun or light shade.

The position depends a great deal on your climate – in warm areas, free from frost problems, they can be treated as free-standing small trees or shrubs, in which case they make magnificent specimen plants. In cooler areas they are best planted against walls, and in very cold regions you may have to forgo the attempt to grow them. The white flowers and grey-green leaves give them a wide range of potential partners, and they would be ideal for a white garden if you are planning one.

Plants can be propagated from seed or cuttings or by layering. Pruning is not required except for general maintenance, such as the removal of any dead branches.

Hoheria glabrata carries the typical white flowers in abundance. Its leaves are smooth and it is supposedly one of the hardiest species.

H. lyallii is similar to the last except that it flowers a little later and has downy leaves.

H. sexstylosa is the most commonly available species; it has similar flowers to the other two but the leaves are shiny and quite narrow. It flowers later than the others.

Hoheria lyallii

Holodiscus discolor

Holodiscus discolor

OCEAN SPRAY

THE ENGLISH NAME FOR this plant is no mistake; the frothing panicles of flowers look just like the white of a breaking wave against the green water of the leaves. It is not seen very often but it is certainly an impressive shrub to grow. The creamy white flowers are held in large feathery plumes during midsummer. This shrub is deciduous and its leaves are a grey green, held on arching branches up to 3m (10ft) tall. It suckers, forming a dense bush, and it is tough enough to take the rigours of most of the winters that it is likely to encounter.

Siting is no problem as this easy-going plant is happy on most soils and will thrive in either sun or light shade, although it possibly prefers the latter.

This looks good either as a single specimen bush or together with several others in a group, particularly if this arrangement has a dark background such as holly or yew. Holodiscus is also suitable as a background to a large herbaceous border.

Propagation may take place either from rooted suckers, removed from around the base of the plant, or from summer cuttings. Any pruning should be undertaken after the plant has flowered.

Holodiscus discolor

Sp (*S*) *A W*
Zone 6

Hydrangea macrophylla 'BLUE WAVE'

Hydrangea

Zone 7

Hydrangea

HYDRANGEA

HYDRANGEAS ARE JUSTLY A very popular garden shrub and yet, curiously, in spite of this people always seem dissatisfied with them; they are always wanting to change their colour. If they have blue ones, they want pink, and vice versa. Perhaps it is the latent creative urge in all of us. I suppose that it is the fact that you can make modifications to the colour that raises these desires. But more of that later; let us first look at the colours as provided.

There are several different and distinct groups. First the mop-head hortensias, possibly the most frequently seen. These have large, rounded heads, as their name suggests, in a range of colours from pink and red to blue. The sterile florets are tightly packed in, with no space between each.

Derived from the same species (*H. macrophylla*) and a few others is the other big group, the lacecaps. These have more elegance than the previous group. Here, the sterile florets are fewer and are arranged mainly round the edge of much smaller fertile buds. Their cool elegance certainly does remind one of lace caps. They are available in a similar colour range to the mop-head hydrangeas except, perhaps, for the darker reds.

The colours of the flowers on both of these two types of hydrangea can be influenced by their environment. On alkaline soil (lime or chalk) the flowers tend to be pink; dig them up and move them to an acid soil and they will change to blue. If you stop on the way and put them into a neutral soil, the colour will also stop midway. This fact can be played upon to change the colour. For example, if you add lime to an acid soil, the colour of your hydrangea will move into the pink. It is not so easy if you live on chalk, but if you hanker after the blue forms it is possible to grow them in containers or raised beds of imported acid soil. You can also buy proprietary "blueing agents", though these work better on neutral soils than on pure chalk.

Other environmental influences are sun and shade. White forms will turn reddish in full sun and in shade many will take on a greenish metallic sheen. Why do we bother with them when they can be so capricious? The answer is simple: they are rewarding plants, no matter what the colour. If kept in good shape the shrubs should not exceed 60-100cm (2-3ft), but they often shoot up to 2m (6ft) and become terribly drawn and untidy.

Hydrangeas have quite large leaves,

Hydrangea arborescens 'GRANDIFLORA'

which can be a good indicator of a plant's water requirements, not only in the hydrangea beds but elsewhere in the garden. As soon as water becomes short hydrangea leaves start to wilt and it is time to get the hose out. They should also be fed to keep them in fine fettle. Other types of hydrangeas include the climbing and the so-called tree forms, which are covered here under the appropriate species names.

Hardiness is something that must be considered. Hydrangeas are reasonably hardy down to −15°C (5°F) and are rarely killed outright, but the new growth can be cut back, reducing the plant to a weak, non-flowering shrub.

As already indicated, hydrangeas are not very fussy about soil, except insofar as it influences the colour of the flowers. They are hungry plants and prefer a rich soil if possible, which should be regularly fed. Light shade is what is required for the best flowering conditions, but a hydrangea will take full sun, although the florets could become a bit blotchy.

These are useful plants for a wide range of situations, including north-facing borders, although I hesitate to mention this, having seen so many miserable-looking specimens in dark, dank corners of cities. Hydrangeas also have the advantage of providing colour during the autumn, and this makes them a good choice for

Hydrangea involucrata 'HORTENSIS'

herbaceous and mixed borders, where they bring a touch of vitality at a time when other plants are dying down.

Propagation from softwood cuttings is simple. Pruning, to many, always seems a mystery. It is left until the spring so that the old branches give extra frost protection to the young growth. Then the flower heads and the oldest wood can be removed. It is possible to cut the whole shrub down, but it will take a season or so to settle back into full flower.

Hydrangea arborescens, Tree Hydrangea, has large, rounded flower heads. These are carried in great profusion from summer to autumn. The shrub grows up to 3m (10ft) or so, and its commonest form is 'ANNABELLE', which has very large flower heads, up to 25cm (10in) across. The shrub itself is smaller than the type-plant and has to a certain extent superseded 'GRANDIFLORA', which has slightly smaller flowers and is of looser habit, though its flowers are still spectacular.

H. aspera is one of the lacecaps, with white or pink outer florets and blue in the centre. It has rough, hairy leaves and a growth of up to 4m (13ft). It is suitable for growing on chalk. The best form is *H.a. villosa*.

Hydrangea macrophylla

Hydrangea sargentiana

H. heteromalla can grow into a small tree of 3m (10ft) or more. It is another lacecap, this time with white flowers that shine out against the dark green leaves in a delicate way. It is available in a number of cultivars.

H. involucrata is a delicate little shrub, rarely exceeding 60-100cm (2-3ft). The lacecap flowers are lilac or rose, with white florets round the outside. It has a form called 'HORTENSIS' (nothing to do with the hortensia hydrangeas, which are the mop-heads), that has double flowers with a redder tinge.

H. macrophylla is the main hydrangea in commerce. It has both mop-head and lacecap cultivars in its ranks. Taking the mop-heads first, it is difficult to be precise about the colours of the various cultivars as the soil can have a great influence and, as has already been explained, they are pink on alkaline soils and blue on acid ones. The forms that follow are some of the best available, with variations: 'ALTONA' (big trusses), 'AMETHYST', 'AMI PASQUIER' (darker colours), 'BLUE PRINCE', 'GÉNÉRAL VICOMTESSE DE VIBRAYE' (free-flowering), 'HAMBURG', 'MADAME EMILE MOUILLIERE' (white), 'PIA' and 'WESTFALEN' (crimson or violet). Of the lacecaps, 'BLUE WAVE' is undoubtedly the most favoured, but in spite of its name this will also be pink on alkaline soils. 'LANARTH WHITE' has white outer florets. The following are good varieties that can be either

pink or blue: 'LILACINA', 'MARIESII', 'VEITCHII' and 'WHITE WAVE' (white outer florets).

H. paniculata has large pyramids of white flowers, somewhat in the manner of lilac. The flowers fade to pink as they begin to pass over. This forms a big bush or a small tree. Its form 'GRANDIFLORA'' has even bigger panicles of flowers, sometimes up to 45cm (1.5ft) in length. 'PRAECOX' flowers earlier.

H. petiolaris is different in that it climbs, though it is still of the lacecap variety. Its flowers are white. It will tolerate quite deep shade and is a very valuable plant to bear in mind for north-facing walls. It can also be used to spread horizontally, as ground cover, and is particularly useful on banks.

H. quercifolia, is becoming popular. As its name suggests, it has leaves shaped like those of the oak, but of a large size. These colour well in the autumn. The flowers are white and, again, in the lacecap form.

H. sargentiana is a large shrub (3m; 10ft) and needs a certain amount of room. The leaves are also large, up to 25cm (10in), and very furry. They colour well in autumn. The flowers have pink or blue centres and white outer florets.

H. serrata is more like one of the mop-heads, with clusters of sterile florets forming compact globular heads in the usual range of pink, blue and white. This is a small shrub, reaching only a metre (3ft). There are several forms available.

Hypericum

ST JOHN'S WORT

THIS IS A VALUABLE genus of shrubs of different heights, all with bright golden yellow flowers. These are in the form of a disk with masses of golden stamens, usually with golden anthers. Flowering continues throughout the summer into autumn. Some later produce bright red or black fruit, the red forms being particularly decorative. The leaves are generally ovate or elliptic and for the most part are retained throughout the winter unless this is severe.

Hypericum

Sp Ⓢ Ⓐ W
Zone 7

Hypericum 'HIDCOTE'

Most hypericums are reasonably hardy and you do not have to worry about them.

Soil tends not to be a problem. Some hypericums have slight difficulties with alkaline soils, though others will grow very happily in ground that is virtually pure chalk. They will tolerate full sun or shade, which can be quite dense in some cases.

The brilliant yellow of hypericum flowers will brighten up any dull spot, particularly as the plants will tolerate some shade. They also do well in mixed borders, giving colour for a long period throughout summer and autumn. The flowers blend happily with other yellows and even with some of the hotter colours. If there is space, hypericums look better in groups. *H. calycinum* makes an excellent ground cover plant, thriving even in comparatively deep shade.

All hypericums grow very easily from late summer cuttings, and the creeping varieties can be divided. The bushier types should be sheared back to the beginning of the last year's growth each spring.

Hypericum calycinum, the Rose of Sharon, is an excellent shrub for ground cover, even in quite shady situations. It only reaches about 30cm (1ft) from the ground and readily spreads by means of underground stems. It has the typical cup-shaped yellow flowers of the hypericum, and it carries these in profusion. It

should be kept out of herbaceous borders as it tends to run riot quickly. It is ideal in shrubberies and wilder areas, and is particularly valuable as an edging to roads or drives. It should be cut almost to the ground every spring to keep it compact.

H. coris is a low, spreading shrub, reaching 30cm (1ft) or slightly more. Its flowers are in clusters 5-12.5cm (2-5in) long. This is a good plant for the larger rock garden or for edging paths.

H. 'HIDCOTE' is probably the most popular of the hypericums, and rightly so. Its 2m (6ft) height is constantly clothed in gold throughout the summer and autumn. If it gets leggy, it can be cut back all over by a third in spring. It is hardy, and even if severe frosts do attack it, it will shoot again from the base – a marvellous plant.

H. inodorum is known mainly by its variety 'ELSTEAD'. The flowers are small and star-like, and are followed by whitish fruit that turn orangey red as they ripen. The species grows up to 1.5m (5ft), but 'ELSTEAD' is of much more dwarf stature. Other berrying forms that are available include 'HYSAN' and 'SUMMERGOLD'.

Hypericum olympicum

H. × *moseranum* is commonly available. This is a short plant up to 60cm (2ft) tall. As well as the usual large golden saucers the flowers have purplish red anthers. It has a form, 'TRICOLOR' that is very popular. The name refers to the leaves, that have green, red, and cream variegations. Some consider this one of the best of the hypericums. Both plants are slightly more tender than the others.

H. olympicum (also known as *H. polyphyllum*) is a dwarf shrub growing less than 30cm (1ft) tall. It is very useful for larger rock gardens or for edging paths. There is a form, 'CITRINUS', that has pale yellow flowers.

H. 'ROWALLANE' has very large flowers, up to 7.5 cm (3in) across. It will make a plant up to 2m (6ft) tall, but it is on the tender side. It will, however, regenerate from the base if cut back by frost.

There is a whole range suitable for the rock garden, some not rising above 2.5cm (1in) from the ground. Without going into further detail, mention should be made of *HH. aegypticum, cuneatum, empetrifolium prostratum, ericoides* and *reptans*.

Indigofera

Sp (S) A W

Zone 8

Hypericum × *moseranum* 'TRICOLOR'

Indigofera heterantha

Indigofera

INDIGO BUSH

THIS IS A VERY large genus of herbs and shrubs, of which a few are in cultivation. As becomes obvious from even a cursory glance at the flowers, these are members of the pea family. The flowers are pink or purple and are held in upright racemes above the finely cut, pinnate leaves. The whole bush gives the impression of airiness and space. This is a summer-flowering shrub that quickly grows to a mature height of about 2m (6ft). It is reasonably hardy, taking frosts down to about −10°C (14°F) or so, though in colder areas it is safer to give it wall protection.

It seems to be happy on a wide variety of soils, including chalk, as long as they are free draining. It prefers full sun.

This is a delightful bush to add an element of lightness to a shrubbery or to fit in well with soft pink, blue or even purple schemes in a mixed or herbaceous border.

Indigoferas can readily be propagated from semi-ripe cuttings. Prune in the same fashion as fuchsias, by cutting back growth in the spring to almost ground level. The plant will flower on new growth.

Indigofera heterantha is by far the commonest species in cultivation, with rich pink flowers continuing from summer well into autumn.

I. potaninii can be found in several nurseries. It has paler flowers and coarser leaves than the preceding.

Itea ilicifolia

Itea

HOLLY-LEAVED SWEETSPIRE

THIS SHRUB PUTS ON quite a show of flowers in the early autumn. Cascades of greeny white flowers tumble down in long chains between the branches of prickly holly-like leaves. These leaves are a glossy green with lighter undersides, and are evergreen. The sweetly fragrant flowers are very small on racemes that can often be up to 30cm (1ft) long. The whole shrub grows up to about 3m (10ft), but it is not especially hardy, only surviving temperatures above −10°C (14°F), so it is another candidate for wall protection in colder areas.

There are no problems with soil, for it will take most types. Itea is happiest in light shade, but will tolerate full sun.

This plant looks good as a specimen grown on its own or in a shrubbery. It is possibly too solid for the herbaceous or mixed border. In milder areas, where it can be free standing, it would make a good screen, hiding an eyesore or shielding part of the garden from view.

Itea ilicifolia is probably the best species and it certainly is the most commonly available. It conforms to the description above, flowering from summer.

I. virginica, Virginia Sweetspire, is quite different. This is a much smaller plant, reaching only 1-1.3m (3-4ft) high, with deciduous leaves that have no prickles and turn red in autumn. The flowers are in shorter, erect panicles rather than the long chains of *I. ilicifolia*. It is hardier than its relative.

Itea

Sp (S) (A) W
Zone 8

Jacaranda

JACARANDA

THESE ARE TROPICAL OR sub-tropical plants, and in colder climates they can only be grown in conservatories or greenhouses. The leaves

Jacaranda

(Sp) S A W
Zone 10

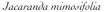

Jacaranda mimosifolia

are bipinnate and somewhat resemble acacia, or mimosa as it is commonly known. Indeed, one of the species is called *J. mimosifolia*, "mimosa-leaved". The blue or violet flowers are trumpet-shaped and hang in clusters. The trees can grow very tall, 15m (50ft) or more in suitable conditions. Although this beautiful tree is, alas, denied to gardeners in colder climates, smaller specimens can be grown under glass, where they can be kept warm during cold winters. They are spectacular and well worth the effort if they can be grown.

The soil should be light and free draining. Sun is essential.

Jacarandas are propagated from half-ripe cuttings in early summer or from seed. No pruning is needed.

Jacaranda mimosifolia (sometimes called *J. ovalifolia*) is one of the widest-grown species. In some areas, for example Pretoria, it is grown as a street tree. It has large blue flowers.

Jasminum humile

Jasminum

Jasminum
Sp (S) (A) (W)
Zone 7

JASMINE

JASMINE IS ONE OF those groups of plants that gardeners always love to have around. They are not necessarily spectacular – comfortable might be a better word – but they tend to do the right thing at the right time. Winter

Jasminum polyanthum

jasmine has flowers in winter, when there is not much else about; common jasmine and some of the others produce a delicious scent on warm evenings. Jasmines are either shrubs with arching stems or climbers, and the latter, if trained, will grow up to considerable heights. The flowers take the form of yellow or white stars on the end of short tubes. The shrubby versions look like broom, with green stems and small trifoliate, almost non-existent, leaves. The climbers have larger, more positive leaves. Several are hardy, taking temperatures down to −14°C (7°F), but others are much more tender and need protection, as much to protect the flower buds as the plant itself. A good flow of air is important, but they all grow well against walls.

They will tolerate most soil conditions and seem to thrive in sun, though they can survive in light shade once they have become established.

Evening fragrance and their ghostly whiteness in the twilight make the scented varieties plants that should be positioned close to the place where one sits out on

Jasminum nudiflorum

summer evenings. Since so many jasmines need to climb up something, a wall near a window seems an ideal place, again where the scent can be appreciated. The winter-flowering jasmine will take a bit more shade and can be placed where it will light up a dull space in winter; for example, against a north wall.

Propagation is from half-ripe cuttings or from layers, and in practice the plants will often self-layer. Pruning should be undertaken after flowering, when most of the flowering stems should be removed, plus any dead or old wood that was forgotten the previous year. So often, jasmine looks like a tangle of dead wood with a few flowering stems.

Jasminum beesianum is a climber, with small red flowers in early summer. The flowers are scented, and are followed by black fruit in autumn.

J. humile is a lax shrub that bears deep yellow, vaguely scented flowers throughout the summer. This also has black berries. 'REVOLUTUM' is the clone normally seen.

J. mesnyi (also known as *J. primulinum*), Primrose Jasmine, is a shrub with bright yellow flowers and is best treated as a climbing form. The flowers are often semi-double. Primrose jasmine is tender, so it requires a mild spot in the open or, alternatively, it must be grown under glass, where it will flower in profusion in early spring. It can be treated as a pot plant and overwintered inside.

J. nudiflorum, Winter Jasmine, is one of the gems of the genus. As its name implies, it is winter flowering, and in this case it really is winter, not the beginning of spring. Its yellow flowers appear throughout all weather. It is hardy but trains well against a wall, even a north one.

J. officinale, Common Jasmine, is another of the gems, mainly due to its wonderful fragrance. The flowers are white and are carried from late summer well into the autumn. It is a rampant climber. There are various forms, including variegated ones.

J. parkeri could hardly be called rampant as it rarely gets above 30cm (1ft) and is eminently suitable for the rock garden. It has yellow flowers.

J. polyanthum is a tenderer version of *J. officinale*, with white, fragrant flowers that appear in late spring. In the open, it certainly needs the protection of a wall to shield the buds, but it makes an excellent plant for the conservatory, where its flowers will open earlier, filling the room with its scent.

Jasminum officinale

Kalmia latifolia

Kalmia

Sp (S) A W

Zone 8

Kalmia

KALMIA

THIS IS A DELIGHTFUL group of plants related to the rhododendron. Kalmia are covered in clusters of shallow cups in a variety of pinks in early summer. The stamens have brown anthers, giving a wonderful, speckled look to the flower, and the overwhelming impression is one of freshness. The leathery leaves are elliptic, and evergreen. There is quite a variation in height between the different species, but the tallest grow up to 3m (10ft). They are reasonably hardy down to −10°C (14°F).

Being part of the Ericaceae, they heartily dislike alkaline soils, and will only grow in the same soils as those in which rhododendrons will flourish. If your soil is alkaline, one way to avoid problems is to place kalmias in containers of peaty soil. They will flourish in light, sun-dappled shade.

These are appropriate plants to grow alongside rhododendrons, where their differing flowering times will give a continuity to the border. Kalmia flowers are more delicate in appearance than those of the rhododendron and can just about be assimilated into the herbaceous border, where they will look good in a pink and purple scheme.

Kalmias can be propagated from seed or firm cuttings in late summer, and they can also be layered. Pruning is restricted to removing spent flower heads and an occasional tidying of the bush.

Kalmia angustifolia, Sheep Laurel, is one of the smaller forms, reaching one metre (3ft) or so. It has deep rose-pink flowers in dense clusters. It is known mainly in its 'RUBRA' form.

K. latifolia, Calico Bush or Mountain Laurel, is the main species in cultivation. It is one of the taller shrubs, with a range of pink flowers, and there are quite a number of cultivars available. 'CLEMENTINE CHURCHILL' is one of the finest forms, with deep red flowers, but the commonest red form available at the moment is 'OSTBO RED'. 'MYRTIFOLIA' is smaller in all its parts, including its pink flowers and leaves. Other attractive varieties are 'ELF', 'BULLSEYE' and 'OLYMPIC FIRE'.

K. polifolia, Bog Myrtle, is a lovely dwarf plant that is totally hardy (coming from Alaska, it has to be). As its name implies, it is used to growing in wet ground, a condition that not many flowering shrubs enjoy. The flowers are a bright pink purple.

Kerria japonica

Kerria

KERRIA

THIS IS A MONOSPECIFIC genus, in other words, it is a genus with only one species: *Kerria japonica*. It is a 2m (6ft) shrub with slender cane-like stems. The flowers are yellow and in the species they are single; in the commonest form in cultivation, however, they are fully double. People seeing the single plant for the first time sometimes find it difficult to realize that it is the same plant. Personally, I find the single flowers far more delicate and desirable than the double. The leaves of both plants are ovate, with heavy veining. Kerria has a tendency to run by underground suckers.

It is perfectly hardy, tolerates most soils, and is happy in either sun or light shade, flowering better in the former.

This is a plant for the shrubbery – insofar as this still exists as a separate area in modern gardens. At the least, it should be planted among other shrubs. Kerria suckers too much and is too erect, certainly in the double form, to fit happily into an herbaceous border.

Plants can be propagated by layering or by dividing off a rooted sucker. Pruning should be undertaken soon after flowering and consists of removing several of the old shoots each year to promote new growth.

'PLENIFLORA' is the commonest variety

Kerria japonica 'PLENIFLORA'

seen. This is a fully double form and is a more erect plant than the single.

'VARIEGATA' (sometimes called 'PICTA') is much more graceful, with wiry arching stems and single flowers. The leaves have a soft variegation of creamy white. This is not such a vigorous plant as other varieties and does not sucker to any extent.

Kerria

Zone 7

Kolkwitzia amabilis

Kolkwitzia

BEAUTY BUSH

THIS IS ANOTHER MONOSPECIFIC genus, *Kolkwitzia amabilis* being its only member. This is a very fine bush, with pretty flowers that appear in great quantity in late spring. The flowers are bell-shaped, pink with yellow in the throat. The leaves are ovate, slightly toothed, with dull green coloration on top and lighter underneath. This is a big bush, quickly growing up to 3m (10ft) high and the same in width, with graceful arching branches. Hardiness should not be a problem outside the Arctic Circle.

Kolkwitzia can take all soils, including

Kolkwitzia

Zone 6

+ *Laburnocytisus adamii*

chalk, as long as they are well drained, and it is perfectly happy in full sun.

This is a good bush to use as a specimen plant or as a member of a shrubbery. It is a bit large for an herbaceous border unless it forms part of the back framework. The colour is easy to place.

Cuttings can be taken at any time of the year. Spent flowering stems and some of the old wood should be pruned away each year immediately after flowering.

Besides the species itself, there is one form commonly available, namely 'PINK CLOUD', which was raised at Wisley. This has deep pink flowers.

+ *Laburnocytisus*

PINK LABURNUM

IF YOU ARE LOOKING for curiosities or simply want to outdo the neighbours, then this is the plant for you, for what you have is a chimaera or graft hybrid. Back in the early nineteenth century a pink broom, *Cytisus purpureus*, was grafted onto a tree of common laburnum, *Laburnum anagyroides*. Both being of the same pea family, the Leguminosae, the graft took. The result was + *Laburnocytisus adamii* which, as expected, had branches of the typical golden rain of the laburnum and arching branches covered in the pink broom. What was not expected were the branches that held flowers intermediate between the two. This was the chimaera. It has had to be propagated vegetatively ever since and is still in cultivation today, with all three types of flower present. This intriguing plant is hardy and takes on the height (7m; 23ft) and shape of the laburnum.

It is happy in most soils as long as they are free draining and prefers full sun.

It is propagated by grafting onto *Laburnum anagyroides* stock. No pruning is required.

The colour combination of pink and yellow is not to everybody's taste and many will prefer the colour and form of the individual plants, but there is no denying that + *Laburnocytisus adamii* stops people in their tracks.

Laburnum

GOLDEN CHAIN TREE

WHO CAN RESIST THE sight of this tree in full flower – if any tree 'drips' with blossom, it is this one. Experiences in childhood have a great influence on taste and I remember a couple of trees from very early school-days that have given me everlasting pleasure in the genus. I can still see now, forty years later, the perfect contrast between the chains of bright yellow flowers, the green trifoliate foliage and the dark glossy stems.

Laburnum × *watereri* 'VOSSII'

Laburnum alpinum

Closer examination of the flowers reveals that this is another member of the pea family, in this case the flowers are produced in long pendulous racemes that brighten up the late spring and summer. It is a tree, not a shrub, and has a good shape, reaching up to 7m (23ft) or more. Laburnum is a very hardy plant and presents no problem with the weather, except that it can be blown over in strong winds. It should be planted in a sheltered position and staked when young. Another problem is that the seeds are poisonous and can be dangerous if there are young children about.

There is no difficulty over soil, as it will

Laburnum

Zone 7

even grow on almost pure chalk. It has a strong preference for full sun but it will take a little light shade.

This is a marvellous tree to plant where it can be silhouetted against a blue sky or against a background of green foliage from other trees. It is also possible to train it over gateways, archways or pergolas, which is a wonderful way to allow the golden chains to hang free. Outside the flowering season, the foliage produces a nice dappled shade.

Laburnums can be propagated from seed, but the best, named forms must be perpetuated by grafting. No pruning is required.

Laburnum alpinum, Scotch Laburnum, is similar to the common laburnum except that it has larger and darker leaves and the flower racemes are longer and denser. It also flowers a bit later, in early summer. It is found most frequently in its form 'PENDULUM', in which not only are the flowers pendulous, but the branches as well, making it a weeping tree.

L. × watereri covers a series of hybrids between *L. alpinum* and *L. anagyroides*. The form 'VOSSII' is one of the best and is certainly the laburnum that is most commonly seen. It has enormous racemes of golden yellow flowers up to 60cm (2ft) long.

Lavandula

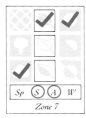

Sp (S) (A) W
Zone 7

Lavandula angustifolia

Lavandula stoechas

Lavandula

LAVENDER

THIS IS ONE OF those nostalgic plants, reminiscent of the cottage garden, that none of us actually remembers. It is the smell that lives in our minds – scent is so much more evocative of forgotten memories than sight; if it were not so, perhaps lavender would not be so popular. However, the hazy blue flower spikes against their grey-leaved background have a lot to offer in the right context. Lavender is not particularly hardy, surviving only down to about −12°C (10°F) or so, but it is not a difficult plant to over-winter in the form of cuttings, so any losses can easily be made good the following year.

There is no problem with choice of soil as long as this is free draining (even this is not essential, I kept a plant alive for years in a spot that regularly flooded after heavy rain, but this is not to be recommended). It must have full sun to do well.

Lavender can be used both formally or informally, but formal uses present problems:

lavenders used for edgings or hedges look fine (to some people) when the bushes are in flower, but awful for the rest of the time – twiggy and uninteresting. Nothing looks worse than a sodden and out-of-season lavender bush. It is better to use lavenders among other plants, where they will be noticed when they are at their best, but where the eye will be drawn elsewhere on their off days. A mixed border, with a continuous structure of plants, is possibly the best place. There certainly is no problem fitting lavenders into most colour schemes – they blend with so many other plants. One advantage of using lavender as a low hedging is that you can run it through your hand as you pass, so planting a bush where this can be done will give a lot of pleasure.

Lavender comes readily from cuttings taken at any time of year. Pruning is not necessary, though the tidy-minded may prefer to trim the old flowering shoots, but lavender does not like being cut back into old wood.

Lavandula angustifolia is the Common Lavender. Unfortunately there is a lot of confusion over naming and you will come across the same plant labelled *L. officinalis*, *L. spica* and *L. spicata* and probably a few other things besides. There are quite a number of forms, of which 'HIDCOTE' and 'MUNSTEAD' are the best and commonest. The former has quite dark flowers, almost purple, rather than the typical lavender blue, and it is a very compact plant growing not much more than 45cm (18in) high. 'MUNSTEAD' is another compact form of the same height, but with lavender-blue flowers. There are several non-lavender forms but these are terribly wishy-washy and are really not worth bothering about. Among these are the pinks, 'HIDCOTE PINK', 'LODDON PINK' and 'ROSEA'. The whites, 'ALBA' and 'NANA ALBA', are not much better.

L. stoechas, French Lavender, is a curiosity. Each flower-stem is topped by a square cone of purple flowers with purple bracts like helicopter rotor-blades, coming out of the top. This is supposedly more tender than *L. angustifolia*, but worth trying.

Lavatera olbia 'ROSEA'

Lavatera

TREE MALLOW

MOST OF THE LAVATERAS are herbaceous, but some are shrubby, growing up to 3m (10ft). The two main ones are quite different in appearance, the only common factor being the typical mallow flower; a flared, pink or purple saucer. Both are coastal plants in the wild and are not very hardy, but will take temperatures down to −7°C (20°F) or so.

No problem with soil: *L. arborea* often grows in pure chalk in the wild. The soil should, however, be free draining, and both species like full sun.

They fit into either shrub or mixed borders, particularly those with a pink or purple theme, but they will also mix with most other colours.

Lavatera arborea is a curious plant with a thick, almost tree-like, stem. The flowers, which are produced in profusion during summer and autumn, are flared, pink trumpets with darker, purple centres. The leaves are soft and hairy, more like those of an herbaceous

Lavatera

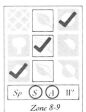

Sp (S) (A) W
Zone 8-9

plant. It is generally propagated from seed, except for the variegated form, 'VARIEGATA', which must be reproduced from cuttings.

L. olbia is a more refined plant, and has pink flowers, with darker veining. It is mainly known in its form 'ROSEA', which is widely available. Like the previous species, this also flowers throughout the summer and autumn. It is propagated from cuttings.

Leptospermum

	✓	✓
✓		
Sp	S	A	W

Zone 9

Leptospermum

MANUKA; TEA TREE

THESE ATTRACTIVE SHRUBS have now spread far beyond the shores of their native Australia and New Zealand, in spite of being somewhat tender in colder areas, preferring temperatures that do not drop below −5°C (23°F). Fortunately, many are quite small, or can be kept small, and can thus be planted in tubs that can be moved for winter protection. They can also be planted against walls, where they will receive some protection.

Leptospermum scoparium 'RED DAMASK'

Leptospermum lanigerum

The flowers are small, and in the form of white, pink or red disks, sometimes with a darker centre. They are carried in great profusion in the late spring and summer. The evergreen leaves are quite small and mainly lanceolate in shape. They used to brew a sort of tea in the New Zealand outback, hence this vernacular name. The height of the bushes can vary considerably. Where conditions suit them they can grow to 5m (16ft) or more, but in cooler areas they are much less vigorous.

They should be provided with light, well-drained soils, and alkaline soils should be avoided. They prefer full sun.

These are very pretty plants and should be seen quite close to, rather than at a distance. With their preference for sheltered positions in cooler areas, they make ideal plants to grow against walls near paths, and they look particularly attractive planted near ceanothus. There is an increasing number of compact forms, suitable for growing in the rock or patio garden.

Leptospermum can be propagated from seed or from semi-hardwood cuttings. Pruning is not necessary except what is needed to keep the plant in bounds, particularly if it is kept in a container of some sort.

Leptospermum humifusum is one of the rock garden forms, growing only 23cm (9in) high. It comes from high altitudes in Tasmania, so it is reasonably hardy, although the foliage occasionally gets cut back in a severe winter. It has white flowers and is widely available.

L. lanigerum (sometimes listed as *L. cunninghamii*, Woolly Tea Tree) has pure white flowers and is considered to be hardier than the more common *L. scoparium*.

L. scoparium, which has fragrant leaves when crushed, is the commonest of the species and an increasing number of cultivars is becoming available. 'CHAPMANII' has rose-pink flowers and bronze leaves. 'KEATLEYI' has white flowers with red markings and dull green foliage. 'NICHOLLSII' has dark red flowers and reddish foliage. 'RED DAMASK' is the most popular with large double, pinky-red flowers and a purplish foliage, and 'SNOW FLURRY' is another double, this time with pure white flowers.

Leycesteria

HIMALAYAN HONEYSUCKLE; ELISHA'S TEARS

THIS IS A CURIOUS plant, with flowers somewhat reminiscent of the shrimp plant (*Belloperone guttata*), though they are not related. Leycesteria has pendulous sprays, with sheaves of bracts from which peep short-tubed flowers. In the case of the shrub, the bracts are crimson and the flowers white. The flowers last from summer into autumn and are followed by gooseberry-like berries. The stems are hollow, similar to canes, and bright green. They rise to about 2-3m (6-9ft). The leaves are a glossy green. It is much planted on pheasant shoots as these birds love the fruit. It

will take temperatures down to about −10°C (14°F). It regenerates freely and quickly from seed, so that any loss is quickly replaced.

Leycesteria is happy on most soils as long as the ground is reasonably fertile and moisture retentive. It must have full sun to show all the colours to their best advantage.

This looks striking as a specimen shrub or planted in groups. It is satisfactory for a large shrubbery but should be kept out of the herbaceous or mixed border as its berries are not only likely to cause masses of seedlings in fertile soil, but will also attract pheasants and other birds that can do damage scratching around.

Propagation from seed or from summer cuttings is very easy. Flowers are borne on new wood so pruning is simple; cut it to the ground in early spring.

The plant normally grown is *Leycesteria formosa* which has been described above. Occasionally one comes across *L. crocothyrsos* which has quite a different flower – a loose terminal raceme with yellow tubular flowers coming out of a short green calyx.

Leycesteria formosa

Leycesteria

Sp (S) (A) W'
Zone 8

Ligustrum lucidum

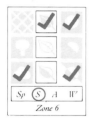

Ligustrum

	✓	✓
✓		✓

Sp (*S*) *A* *W*

Zone 6

Ligustrum

PRIVET

WHAT, YOU MAY WELL ASK, is a dull, leggy hedge plant doing in a book on flowering trees and shrubs? In fact there are nearly 20 different varieties of privet currently available, any one of which makes a fine free-standing specimen or a member of the shrub garden. All have frothing panicles of white flowers, with a fragrance that most people find revolting, though a few enjoy it. The flowers appear in late summer and are followed by black berries. The foliage is generally ovate and not of any great interest, except that there are several much more exciting varieties that have variegated or golden coloration. If left to its own devices, privet can grow to 6m (20ft) or more, but it is easily trimmed. It is generally as hardy as it needs to be for most climates.

As its universality as a hedging plant shows, privet has few problems with most soils. It will also stand sun or light shade, though it can get very leggy if the latter is too deep.

Privets can be grouped to most attractive effect in a shrub garden, and the golden and variegated forms are excellent for lightening a dull patch, particularly in winter.

Plants can be propagated very easily from cuttings at most times of year. Prune as much or as little as you like: shrubs just need to be kept tidy; hedges must be cut back regularly. Flowers are produced on old wood, so regular trimming is likely to inhibit them, but plants will regenerate if cut to the ground in order to restart a hedge.

Ligustrum japonicum 'ROTUNDIFOLIUM' has round leaves crowded on the stems. These are slightly deformed, so that they look like young box leaves on a larger scale.

L. lucidum has some very good variegated forms: 'EXCELSUM SUPERBUM' has deep yellow and creamy white mottling, while 'TRICOLOR' has the same markings plus a pinkish margin.

L. ovalifolium is one of the plants normally used for hedging, but it has some interesting varieties. 'ARGENTEUM' has pale creamy white variegations round the margins. 'AUREUM' has rich golden leaves, with just a bit of green in the centres. Both of these varieties are excellent for lightening dark places, but their light colour means that the flowers are not

Ligustrum vulgare

particularly conspicuous.

L. quihoui and the next species are the best flowering forms, with this one taking the prize: it has large, loose panicles of flowers up to 25cm (10in) long and it is deciduous.

L. sinense is another good flowering species, but this time it also has a good variegated form, 'VARIEGATUM'.

L. × vicaryi deserves a mention because of its excellent light golden foliage, though its flowers are no better than any of the others.

L. vulgare, Common Privet, is another of the hedging privets, but if left to grow freely it will produce masses of white flowers. There are several forms, including golden ones.

Liriodendron

TULIP TREE

A SMALL GENUS OF two species, one from China and the other, *Liriodendron tulipifera*, from North America, the tulip tree is closely related to the magnolias. The flowers consist of six upright petals, fashioned like the tulip from

Liriodendron tulipifera

which it takes its name, and three reflexed sepals. These are solitary, on the ends of the branches, and appear in summer. The colour of the flowers is yellowish green. The leaves are quite large and are three-lobed with the central one chopped off, giving the tree the appearance that large insects have been munching away at every leaf. These magnificent trees can get very tall given the right conditions – an eventual height of 30m (100ft) is by no means unusual and in the wild they can reach twice as high. There seems to be no problem with hardiness.

A tulip tree must have deep rich soil. This is not only for its nutritional needs, but because a tree of this height needs plenty of deep roots. It also likes full sun.

A tree to plant for future generations, it will take quite a number of years to get established and possibly even longer before it flowers. Flowers may occasionally be seen on trees that are five or six years old, but in most cases it is necessary to wait much longer. Its sheer size bars it from most gardens, and even if you can accommodate it, you still need the room to stand back and enjoy its beauty.

Tulip trees will come readily from seed. Young plants can be layered. Varieties are grafted onto seedling stock.

Liriodendron tulipifera has several varieties of which two are generally available: 'AUREO-MARGINATUM' has yellow margins to the leaves, while 'FASTIGIATUM' is the same as the species except that it is more columnar in shape.

L. chinense, the Chinese species, is occasionally seen. It is not as big as the American tree either in its stature or in the flowers. The petals of the latter are also less upright and more open. *L. chinense* is perfectly hardy.

Liriodendron

Sp (S) *A* (W)
Zone 6

Lonicera

HONEYSUCKLE

MANY GARDENERS ARE OFTEN surprised when they discover the number and variety of honeysuckles. The one that really comes as a surprise is *Lonicera nitida*, which is very

Lonicera

Sp (S) *A* (W)
Zone 5-8

commonly used as a hedging plant (it has very small oval leaves and is sometimes mistakenly called privet). This does flower, but very insignificantly, so we will leave it and move on to the more floriferous varieties, of which there are basically two types; those that climb and those that are bushes. They all have tubular flowers with a lip. The tube varies in length, the climbing species mainly having the longest, and the colour varies considerably from yellow to red, with white and pink in attendance. Not mentioned so far is the wonderful fragrance that is particularly noticeable in the evening. I adore it, but alas I seem to be allergic to it. One sprig in my study and I start suffering from a type of hay fever. Every year, out of sheer hedonism, I decide to suffer for a few evenings just to enjoy it. That honeysuckle is fragrant is not news to many people, but perhaps not everyone is aware that there are fragrant varieties that flower in winter. The height varies: the climbing varieties disappear out of sight through tall trees; the shrubby ones rise to about 3m (10ft) or so. Honeysuckles are completely hardy and should have no problems, even in the worst winters.

Lonicera × tellmanniana

There are no difficulties over soil conditions, for honeysuckles will grow almost anywhere. Sun or light shade makes little difference, except that most undoubtedly flower better in full sun, though some actually prefer light shade.

This is a group of shrubs and climbers that can be put virtually anywhere, though some varieties will climb trees and shrubs and kill them. They mix in with most kinds of borders, and even climbing varieties can be grown up tripods to great effect. They can also be grown over archways and gateways, where the scent can be appreciated in passing. For similar reasons, a wall near an opening window is a good position, and this would be equally suitable for some of the shrubby varieties.

Propagation is from seed or half-ripe cuttings. Pruning is needed to keep everything tidy: dead wood should be cut out and some of the old wood should be removed from shrubby species every year.

Lonicera × americana is a climbing species, with very fragrant, pinkish yellow flowers that are purple in bud. This is a good vigorous form that looks well grown on a tripod in an herbaceous or other border. It flowers in midsummer.

L. × brownii is a beautiful climbing form with fine orange and scarlet flowers, although

Lonicera tragophylla

it lacks scent. 'DROPMORE SCARLET', a superior form with a longer flowering period, is widely available. The form 'FUCHSIOIDES' is a brilliant scarlet.

L. caprifolium is another climber, this time with flowers of creamy white. It is a very good scented species and has a form, 'PAUCIFLORA', with small, pink-tinged flowers.

L. fragrantissima is a shrubby honeysuckle that flowers during the winter. The flowers are creamy white and scented. They are quite small and are borne on almost leafless branches, as the plant is only semi-evergreen. Unlike any other winter-flowering shrubs, this forms quite a large bush, up to 3m (10ft) high. It should not be planted in the forefront of a border as it can look rather boring during the summer.

L. × heckrottii is halfway between a shrub and a climber. It is in fact a shrub, but its stems are so weak that it is best to secure them to a wall or framework. The flowers are yellow with a pinkish tinge to the lips, and although a cultivar, 'GOLD FLAME', is often listed, this seems to be the same as the type-plant.

L. henryi is a vigorous climber with good

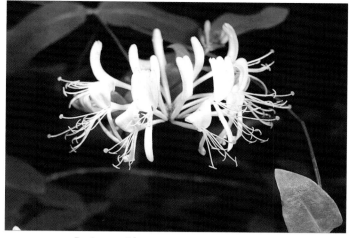

Lonicera periclymenum

Lonicera periclymenum 'BELGICA'

foliage. The flowers are purplish red and appear in midsummer.

L. involucrata is one of the shrubby varieties. It has curious yellow flowers surrounded by red bracts that appear as the flower fades.

L. japonica, Japanese Honeysuckle, is an evergreen climber. The fragrant flowers are white, turning yellow, often with a reddish blush. It has two forms of importance: 'AUREO-RETICULATA' has distinctive leaves, many (but not all) of which are shaped like oak leaves, with a yellow veining, while 'HALLIANA' is a very fragrant variety. This last is more tender than most honeysuckles, so it appreciates wall protection.

L. periclymenum, Common Honeysuckle, is the British honeysuckle that, because of its fragrance, has probably been in cultivation for a long time. The flowers are white and yellow, sometimes with a reddish tinge. Several good forms are in cultivation and widely available. 'BELGICA' (also known as Early Dutch Honeysuckle) has purple-red flowers fading to a pink yellow. 'SEROTINA' (or Late Dutch Honeysuckle) is a much deeper shade of purple, fading to pink. As its second name implies it flowers later than the previous variety.

L. pileata is included, not because of its flowers, but for its shiny blue berries and the fact that it makes excellent ground cover in a shrub border or along a drive. It is a bush form with a great spread.

L. × tellmanniana is a deciduous climber that has wonderful bright yellow flowers with an orange tinge. It thrives in shade.

L. tragophylla is one of the parents of the previous plant. Its bright yellow flowers are the largest of any honeysuckle, but although this is one of the showiest species, it is not scented.

Magnolia

Zone 8

Magnolia

MAGNOLIA

THE WORLD WOULD BE a much poorer place without magnolias, certainly a less attractive one. These glorious flowers are one of the few really exotic-looking blossoms that can be grown in the open in colder areas. The chalices of pure white, sometimes tinged with pink, held up against a blue sky or against large glossy leaves are a sight that can be breath-taking. Not all the forms have flowers that emulate chalices, many have strap-like petals, some quite narrow, some pendent rather than upright. In some species the flowers appear before the leaves, creating an incredible display of white or pink; in others,

Magnolia grandiflora

Magnolia kobus

they appear after the leaves and are beautifully set off by them. Most are deciduous, but there are notable exceptions, particularly *M. grandiflora*, which has large elliptical leaves that are very glossy on their upper surfaces.

With the number of varieties available, it is possible to have one or another flowering from late winter through into the autumn. Consideration must be given to height when buying magnolias. Some of the trees can grow to a considerable height and are totally unsuitable for the small garden, but there are many of the shrubby varieties that are perfect for this type of location. Another consideration is the length of time you must wait before the plant flowers: again, some of the tree varieties can take up to 20 years or more, so they are not ideal plants for someone who is likely to move on in a few years unless that person is completely altruistic (fortunately there are such people). Hardiness should not be too much of a problem, as most will take a certain degree of frost – down to −12°C (10°F) – but the plants should be shielded from cold winds in order to protect the flowers.

Most will tolerate a wide range of soils, but although most will put up with slightly alkaline soils, a number of species dislike any alkalinity. Most will put up with either full sun or light shade. Varieties that flower towards the end of winter should be planted away from

Magnolia stellata

the early morning sun, as this may ruin frosted blooms by thawing them out too rapidly.

Magnolias should not be grown as part of an herbaceous or mixed border unless you can guarantee not to dig around the roots. These extend some way from the plant, and magnolias resent any form of disturbance. Lawns make an excellent place for specimen trees and shrubs, not only from the visual point of view but because the roots are unlikely to receive any disturbance. The question of root disturbance is not the only problem when considering associations: magnolias are truly specimen plants and it is difficult to mix them visually with other plants. If they are not in grass, it is possible to underplant them with something else that is rarely disturbed, such as cyclamen.

Propagation is from layering or from seed, but inferior forms may be raised from the latter. Grafting onto seedling stock can be a safe way for named forms. Young plants should be planted out in spring. Avoid autumn, as damaged roots will not be able to recover during the winter and are likely to rot. No pruning is required but some enthusiasts recommend dead-heading if possible to prevent prolific seed production sapping the vitality of the plant.

Nearly all the available magnolias, and there are a lot, are well worth having. The following list describes just a few of them.

Magnolia campbellii is a magnificent plant that flowers from the late winter into spring, before its leaves open. It is a large tree and unfortunately it is one of those that takes at least 20 years to flower, and even then frost can destroy a year's flowering. The flowers are shaped like tulips – goblets is the normal description. They are a dark, rose pink, paler on the inside. This magnolia needs a protected spot if it is to flower well. There are several different forms available.

Magnolia × soulangiana

M. denudata (also called *M. heptapeta*) is a very beautiful pure white magnolia, with broad waxy petals. Its flowers appear in early spring and have a fine lemon scent. It forms a small dome-shaped tree and is suitable for the medium-sized garden.

M. grandiflora must be the best of the lot; some would say the best of all flowering plants. The flowers are great open dishes, 23-25cm (9-10in) across, of pure creamy white, with a white central boss, and they have a lemon fragrance. The evergreen leaves are equally magnificent: shaped like large laurel leaves, they are dark green and very glossy, and in some varieties the underside is felted in brown. This species is not particularly tender, but it looks and thrives better against a wall, preferably a tall wall, as the tree can get very large over the years. The buds open over a long period from midsummer well into autumn.

The big disadvantage is that you have to wait 20 years or so for the first flowers. Fortunately, some of the new forms are much quicker to mature, more than halving the waiting time. 'EXMOUTH' is one of these varieties. This has a brownish felt on the underside of the leaves and the tree is more

upright in character. 'FERRUGINEA' again has a rusty felted back to its leaves. 'GOLIATH' has enormous flowers up to 30cm (1ft) across. It starts to flower relatively early in its life, possibly earlier than any other form.

M. × *highdownensis* has white hanging flowers. These have a red central boss of stamens and are fragrant. Apart from the flower, the main point of interest is that this species is suitable for growing on chalk.

M. kobus is a fairly tall tree with white fragrant flowers. The flowers are relatively small, only 10cm (4in) across. The age at which this species flowers is very variable but it is not unusual for it to take at least twelve years.

M. macrophylla, Great-leaved Magnolia, is a tall tree, up to 15m (50ft), with enormous leaves up to one metre (3ft) long and 30cm (1ft) wide. The flowers are creamy white and also very large; up to 30cm (1ft) wide.

M. quinquepeta (also known as *M. liliiflora*) flowers in late spring after its leaves have appeared. The flowers are rosy purple on the outside and much paler inside. It is not a very big shrub (4m; 13ft), which makes it a good plant for the smaller garden. Its form 'NIGRA' is a deeper purple in colour.

M. sieboldii has hanging fragrant flowers that are white, this time with a central boss of reddish stamens. It forms a medium-sized shrub (5m; 16ft) and flowers from the age of

Magnolia × highdownensis

about four or five years.

M. sinensis is one of the pendent forms, with saucers of white flowers and red stamens. These flowers are borne in summer and have the lemon scent that is characteristic of so many magnolias.

M. × soulangiana has big upright, goblet flowers of white, or pale pink slightly stained with purple, particularly at the base. The flowers appear in early spring, before the leaves. This hybrid can get quite tall (10m; 30ft), and there are many varieties from which to choose, most varying slightly in the size and colour of the flowers.

M. stellata is a magnolia with which many people are familiar as it is frequently seen in small gardens. It is a small shrub, though it will eventually grow up to nearly 3m (10ft), and in spring it is covered in white flowers that are composed of many strap-like petals. These appear before the leaves come and continue for quite a long time. This species is sometimes sold as a form of *M. kobus*, to which it is related. It is easy to grow, flowers while still quite young, and is ideal for the first-time buyer.

M. wilsonii is another form with white hanging flowers. These are scented and have a red boss of stamens. This magnolia flowers in summer and will stand a bit of shade.

Mahonia

OREGON GRAPE

THE CLARITY OF ITS colour and the fresh, almost astringent, smell of its flowers, which appear in winter or early spring, make this a most appealing plant. The sulphur yellow flowers are either held in erect spikes or flop lazily over the leaves. These are followed later in the year by black or purple berries. The large leaves are themselves fascinating. They are pinnate, with the leaflets in most of the forms being quite prickly. The colour varies from dark glossy green to matt light green, and although mahonias are evergreen, the leaves also turn purple in autumn. The species vary in height but generally form bushes up to

Mahonia japonica

about 2m (6ft). On the whole they are fairly hardy and should cause few problems.

There seem to be no restrictions on the type of soil in which mahonias will thrive. They will accept full sun or, in some cases, quite deep shade.

These beautiful plants are useful for bringing the garden alive during the winter, particularly in dark corners, where the flowers stand out. They can be planted on the north side of buildings or fences, and their glossy foliage can be used as a background to accent other plants later in the season.

Propagation is from rooted suckers, half-ripe cuttings or even seed, although the latter will not come true. No pruning is necessary beyond what is needed to keep the plant tidy and the removal of some of the older naked wood to rejuvenate the shrub.

Mahonia aquifolium, Oregon Grape, is one of the commonest species seen. This is a small suckering bush with fragrant yellow flowers in late winter. The dark green, glossy foliage turns purple in the autumn. There are several forms available from nurseries, including 'APOLLO', which has the merit of not suckering as badly as the others, and 'ATROPURPUREA',

Mahonia

Sp S A W
Zone 7

97

which has leaves that turn a rich reddish purple in autumn and winter.

M. bealei has a mixed reception these days – many gardeners feel that it has been superseded by *M. japonica* while others still believe that its enormous leaves and its erect flowers have a lot to offer.

M. japonica has large racemes of flowers that are more pendulous and spreading than those of the previous species. As with most mahonias, they are very fragrant.

M. lomariifolia is a taller bush, up to 3m (10ft) high, with large clusters of erect spikes appearing over very large leaves.

M. × *media* is the general name given to a whole series of extremely good hybrids between *M. japonica* and *M. lomariifolia*. 'BUCKLAND' flowers in the late autumn and continues well into winter. In this and in 'CHARITY', the latter being possibly the best of the hybrids, the flowers start erect and droop as they age. 'LIONEL FORTESCUE' has the advantage of upright spikes, and the bush is more spreading. 'WINTER SUN' has semi-erect racemes on a compact bush.

M. 'UNDULATUM' is similar to *M. aquifolium* in many respects but it is much taller, with wavy-edged leaves and deep yellow flowers.

Malus floribunda

Crab apples are adaptable to most soil conditions. They prefer full sun, although they may sometimes do reasonably well in light shade.

These are specimen trees that can be planted at the back of borders or on lawns. They look delightful on lawns, and cast a reasonable amount of dappled shade in which to sit on summer days, but the falling apples can make a mess. A crab apple can look attractive in a cottage garden situation, with plants crowded around its base.

Propagation is undertaken by grafting

Malus

Sp S A W
Zone 6

Malus

CRAB APPLES

THESE TREES ARE USEFUL on two counts: their blossom in spring and their fruit in autumn. Although this book is chiefly about flowering trees and shrubs, one has to take into account the other attributes that a genus may possess. Most people tend to grow crab apples for their colourful fruit and it comes as a pleasant surprise to realize how attractive the blossom can be. This is a typical apple blossom, in white, varying shades of pink or even red. The flowers appear in the spring on trees that are generally a suitable size for even a small garden. They are very hardy and need little protection, other than from cold winds. Late frost can damage the blossom.

Malus 'PROFUSION'

Malus 'LADY NORTHCLIFFE'

suitable material onto apple stock. Plants can be raised from seed, but the results will be very variable. Pruning should be the same as for fruiting apple trees: the centre should be kept open, and any dead or weak growth removed. Generally, the tree should be kept tidy and in shape, and there will be no problem with regeneration if it is cut too hard.

A number of varieties are grown with scant regard for their blossom. These are usually very good fruiting forms, but in spite of this quality they are largely ignored in the following list.

Malus baccata has large white flowers and red fruit.

M. 'ELEYI' is red-purple in all its parts: flowers, leaves and fruit.

M. floribunda is a profusely flowering form with pale pink flowers emerging from red buds. It has yellow fruit.

M. hupehensis has flowers that are pink fading to white and are fragrant. The fruit is yellow tinged with red. This can become a tall tree, reaching up to 9m (30ft).

M. 'LADY NORTHCLIFFE' has white blossom, opening from red buds. It has yellow fruit.

M. 'LEMOINEI' has good reddish-purple flowers and purple leaves and fruit.

M. 'PROFUSION' is another deep-pink-flowered, purple-leaved tree. The fruit is a similar colour.

M. 'ROYALTY' is a gorgeous colour. It has red flowers set off against purple leaves. Even the fruit is a purple colour when it appears.

M. tschonoskii has pink flowers fading to white. The fruit is yellow tinged with purple.

Melaleuca

Sp S A W
Zone 10

Melaleuca

MELALEUCA

THIS IS A LARGE GENUS of evergreen trees and shrubs, mainly from Australia. They are related to the bottlebrushes and the banksias and are similar in that it is the bundles of stamens that give the flowers their charm. The flower heads are either round or in small cylindrical spikes, and are smaller and less brash than those of their relatives. With the exception of blue, they come in a complete range of colours. The leaves of many species are fragrant when crushed. Melaleuca range up to 25m (80ft) in height, but it is usually the smaller shrubby species that are the most garden-worthy. They will only grow outside in areas that are frost-free; the smaller plants

Melaleuca hypericifolia

can be grown in a warm conservatory.

Melaleuca will tolerate a wide range of soil types and will even put up with drought conditions. They prefer full sun. The flowers range in colour from mauve to crimson, so it is possible to select a species to suit virtually any scheme for a mixed or shrub border.

The flowers benefit from close inspection, so melaleucas should not be planted too far back in the border. The smaller bushes make good plants for conservatories, from where they can be moved outside during the warmer summer months.

Propagation is from seed or summer cuttings. Pruning is restricted to a light cutting-back of the shrubby species after flowering, in order to keep them compact.

Melaleuca decussata is known as the Totem-pole Honey Myrtle and grows up to 3m (9ft) high. This is a dark green shrub with mauve-lilac flowers, which appear throughout the summer.

M. fulgens, the Scarlet Honey Myrtle, has, as its name implies, bright scarlet flowers. These appear in the late spring and make the plant one of the showiest of the genus. It will grow up to 3m (9ft), but can be kept more compact by regular pruning.

M. hypericifolia, Hillock Bush, is quite a fast growing bush of 3m (9ft) or so. It carries flowers of red stamens in spring. The leaves are strongly aromatic if crushed.

M. incana is a graceful shrub noted for its fine silver-green leaves, which take on a tinge of purple in the winter. The flowers are whitish yellow and are carried in the spring. The shrub can grow up to 3m (9ft), but is often smaller.

M. lateritia, Robin Redbreast, has brick-red flowers that appear over a very long season, from late spring well into summer. It is a tall and graceful shrub, growing to 3m (9ft) high, with fine, linear leaves.

M. steedmanii is a small shrub of up to a metre to 2m (3 to 6ft). It has bright crimson flowers in the early spring.

These are just a few plants from the large genus of 100 or more species: it is well worth going to nurseries to look at the many others that are available.

Nerium

OLEANDER

THIS IS A GENUS of three species, of which *Nerium oleander*, a plant of Mediterranean origin, is justly regarded as a splendid long-flowering plant for frost-free areas. This is an evergreen shrub reaching up to 4m (13ft), and with training it can be grown as a standard. The sweetly-fragrant flowers are tubular, with wide, flared mouths, and they can be single or double. The colours range from white, pink and red to pale yellow. In warmer areas there is quite a range of cultivars available. Oleanders are frost tender and should only be grown outside in warmer areas, but they make suitable subjects for containers and are excellent conservatory plants that can be moved outside during the summer.

Any soil will be acceptable, but they prefer a well-drained position in full sun.

Propagation is from half-ripe wood in late summer. No pruning is generally required, but if an oleander is to keep a good dense habit it should be cut back quite hard every few years to promote growth.

Nerium

Zone 10

Nerium oleander

Nerium oleander

Olearia

DAISY BUSH

GARDENERS HAVE MIXED FEELINGS about daisy bushes. When they are in flower, they are an incredible sight – the whole surface of the bush is covered in flowers. Out of season, alas, they take on a drab quality that is hard to disguise. The flowers, which are fragrant in a few species, are typical daisies, with a central yellow disk and ray-like petals in white, pale blue or pale pink. The evergreen leaves are a soft grey-green with a felted underside. The bushes rarely have any shape to them and they are not all that hardy, taking frosts only down to −7°C (20°F) or so. On the other hand, they are salt tolerant and grow well beside the sea.

There are no problems with the type of soil as long as it is free draining. Olearia prefers to be grown in full sun.

This bush does well in a shrub or mixed border, where its profuse flowering can be seen but where it does not draw attention to itself after flowering. An olearia can grow up to 3m (10ft), so there is quite a lot to hide.

Olearias are propagated from summer cuttings. After flowering the unsightly seed

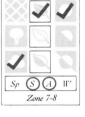

Olearia

Zone 7-8

heads can be sheared off. Some of the old wood can be removed to promote new growth, and the plant will respond well to being cut back hard if necessary.

Olearia × haastii carries masses of white flowers in the early autumn but is dreary for the rest of the year. It is the commonest form available and is reasonably hardy.

O. macrodonta is also widely available. It also has masses of white flowers, and its soft holly-like leaves are of more interest than those of the previous plant. This species grows well by the sea, and there is a 'MAJOR' and a 'MINOR' form.

O. × mollis has large white flowers and silver-grey foliage. It is one of the more compact olearias.

O. nummularifolia has small, fragrant, off-white flowers, appearing in late summer.

O. phlogopappa (what a lovely name!), sometimes called *O. stellulata*, flowers earlier, in spring. It has white flowers and aromatic foliage. Several varieties of this species are available, ranging in colour from pale shades of blue to pink and mauve.

O. × scilloniensis is absolutely covered with white flowers in late spring or early summer.

O. semidentata is a fast-growing bush when in a suitable position. It has the largest daisies of the family, up to 5cm (2in) across. These are violet with a darker centre.

Osmanthus

Olearia semidentata

Olearia × haastii

Osmanthus

OSMANTHUS

THIS IS A WONDERFUL group of evergreen shrubs, once considered part of the genus *Helichrysum*, that can form the backbone of a shrub border or fit in well with other plants. They can also be used to make a good thick hedge. The flowers are relatively small, but they are borne in great profusion and have a delightfully fragrant scent. The flowers are trumpet-shaped and are white. The leaves are evergreen and, in the main, glossy. The bushes can grow quite large, up to 4m (13ft), though they can be kept to a small size by pruning. On the whole Osmanthuses are quite hardy, taking temperatures down to at least −15°C (5°F).

There does not seem to be any problem with the type of soil that they require, but like most plants they prefer a fertile soil if they are to flourish. They are happiest in sun, but will take light shade.

These shrubs are covered in a mass of white flowers and are scented, two factors to take into account when siting them in the garden. The mass of white will show at a distance, particularly against the darker green-leaved forms, but individual flowers will not stand out. The scent travels but it is nice to have it at hand, or rather at nose. Osmanthus can be successfully used as a hedging plant, so in a smaller garden it might screen some eyesore or divide off part of the garden, provided that it is positioned somewhere that people regularly pass, so that the individual flowers and their scent receive their due share of appreciation. It will also fit in a shrub border.

Osmanthus can be propagated from half-ripe cuttings taken in early summer. The bushes need no pruning but some benefit from being shorn over after flowering. This not only keeps the shrub compact, but increases the next season's flowering.

Osmanthus × *burkwoodii* (sometimes called × *Osmarea burkwoodii*) comes into bloom in the early spring, producing numbers of white, scented flowers. It has ovate, glossy leaves. It benefits from a trim after flowering.

O. decorus flowers in early spring and is more spreading than some of the other species.

O. delavayi is one of the parents of *O. burkwoodii* and shares most of its attributes, including increased flowering potential after a trim. It is reputed to be hardier than *burkwoodii*, but I feel that this is of little consequence in most areas since the latter can take −15°C (5°F) without a hint of discomfort. It flowers at the same time as its offspring and is a good hedging plant.

O. fragrans (Sweet Olive) is a favourite in gardens in warmer climates because of its very

Osmanthus delavayi

strong scent. It flowers in early spring and is very tender, needing a frost-free climate. It can, however, be grown as a conservatory plant in a tub.

O. heterophyllus (also known as *O. ilicifolius*) has very small flowers. These are hard to see, but you know they are there by their sweet scent. The plant has two other bonuses besides the scent: it flowers in October, when not much else is happening, and it has very good foliage. The general shape of the leaves is like that of holly (hence the old name *ilicifolius* – *ilex* is holly, *folius* is leaf), but the shape and the colour vary in the cultivars available: 'AUREOMARGINATA' has golden yellow edge-markings; 'PURPUREUS' has purple leaves, turning greener as they age, and 'VARIEGATUS' has a white edging to the leaves. This species also makes a good hedging plant.

Osmanthus × *burkwoodii*

Ozothamnus

OZOTHAMNUS

ALSO KNOWN AS helichrysums, *Ozothamnus ledifolius* and *O. rosmarinifolius* are both Australian shrubs. The former would be among my favourites, if I were bold enough to try to compile such a list. As a general description, they are evergreen, with small, needle-like

Ozothamnus

	✓	✓
✓		
Sp	S	A	W

Zone 8

Ozothamnus rosmarinifolius

Paeonia

Sp (S) A W

Zone 7

look that lasts for most of the year. The flowers appear a reddish brown in bud, opening to white. The fluffy seed heads are an off-white, buff colour. The yellow stripe under the leaves is a volatile exudate which makes the bush very vulnerable to fire. In its native Tasmania it is known as the 'KEROSENE BUSH'.

O. rosmarinifolius again has linear leaves, this time very similar in shape and colour to rosemary, from which it gets its name. The overall impression is of a soft blue-green. The flowers open pinkish white from red buds.

Paeonia

TREE PEONY

PEONIES ARE GENERALLY THOUGHT of as herbaceous plants but there are a few good shrubby species that are suitable for any garden. These have typical peony flowers in yellow and red, set off by deeply cut foliage. The flowers appear in early summer, but unfortunately do not have a very long season. The shrubs grow quite tall, some reaching up to 2.25m (7ft), and take temperatures down to at least −14°C (7°F).

Tree peonies are happy in most soils, as long as they are free draining, and will take

Paeonia lutea 'LUDLOWII'

leaves. They are attractive in so many ways: the tips of the fresh young growth, the flower buds, the flowers, and even the fluffy seed heads, all give these plants quality for most of the year. The flowers are very small but in tight flat-headed bunches, so they show up well against the green foliage. Ozothamnuses are not very tall, growing up to 1.25m (4ft), and they can be kept shorter, although I see no reason why anyone would want to do this. They are reasonably hardy, and they could take temperatures down to −10°C (14°F) in a well-sheltered position.

These plants seem to tolerate most soils, as long as they are free draining, but they prefer full sun and a sheltered position, away from strong winds.

They have so much to contribute that they should be planted near a path, where they can be seen regularly. They can also be planted as a group or as specimen plants.

They can easily be raised from summer cuttings. Pruning is not necessary but bushes can be cut back heavily if required.

Ozothamnus ledifolius has green, needle-like leaves, with a yellow stripe on the underside. This, plus the yellow of the new growth and bracts, gives the bush a very fresh

both full sun or a little light shade.

These make fine specimen shrubs, particularly if planted in a group. They are also an attractive plant to grow at the back of an herbaceous border, where their flowers give interest and colour early in the season and the foliage continues to provide background support after the flowers have faded. Their main disadvantage is the short duration of the blooms, which makes it hard to justify planting these peonies in a small garden.

They can be propagated from the seed that is copiously provided each autumn in the form of small black fruit held in pods. Pruning is undertaken in early spring, when some of the old wood is removed to encourage new growth. In some areas, this new growth may need protection from any late severe frosts.

P. delavayi has very deep, rich red flowers and a boss of golden anthers. Slightly shorter in stature than the others, it tends to sucker, though not to the extent that this becomes a nuisance.

P. × lemoinei is a series of hybrids, raised by crossing *P. lutea* and *P. suffruticosa*. They have some of the biggest of the tree peony flowers – 17-20cm (7-8ins) across with colours in various shades of yellow, sometimes with red or orange markings. The flowers of some forms are double or semi-double.

P. lutea has golden flowers. It has a form,

Paeonia suffruticosa 'ROCK'S VARIETY'

'LUDLOWII', which is seen more frequently than the species. This has larger flowers than *P. lutea* and the shrub itself is also bigger.

P. suffruticosa, Moutan, has large flowers in a range of colours from pink and red, to white and yellow. These sometimes have markings in a second colour and can be found in semi-double and double as well as the single forms. Notable is 'ROCK'S VARIETY' with its huge white flowers blotched at the base.

Paeonia suffruticosa

Paeonia delavayi

Perovskia

Zone 7

Perovskia

RUSSIAN SAGE

THE NAME MAY BE unfamiliar, but once this plant has been seen it is not easily forgotten. To give some form of visual context, it could be said to look like a shrubby form of nepeta but with a brighter blue flower. It is a small (1m; 3ft) airy shrub, with each branch end covered in a spray of small lavender-blue flowers at the right time of year. The leaves are a soft grey, complementing the blue beautifully. Perovskia flowers from the late summer into autumn. There is not much problem with hardiness as it will stand at least −14°C (7°F).

Perovskias will take a range of soils as long as they are well drained, but full sun is essential.

This is a wonderful plant to include in the herbaceous or mixed border (as it is cut to the ground each year, it is very much of an herbaceous nature). The clouds of blue fit in with the softer colour schemes, particularly with blues, mauves and pinks, and it is an ideal plant to give a bit of sudden, but not too violent, colour in a silver garden.

Perovskia is propagated from summer cuttings. It is pruned each spring almost to ground level.

P. atriplicifolia is the main species found in cultivation and has been described above. There is a form, 'BLUE SPIRE', that is probably more common than the species itself. This has larger panicles of flowers.

Philadelphus

MOCK ORANGE

THIS IS A WONDERFUL genus of shrubs for the garden. The pleasure lies in the pure or creamy white flowers that are borne in profusion during the summer and in their glorious scent. The flowers are mainly single but there are also several double varieties. Philadelphus is a deciduous shrub with medium-sized, ovate leaves, whose coloration, mainly of lighter greens, sets off the white flowers to charming effect. The shrubs vary considerably in height, ranging from a few metres up to 5m (16ft). They are all hardy enough for gardeners not to have to worry about protection of any kind.

There are no problems with choice of soil, for philadelphuses will thrive on almost any type as long as it is reasonably fertile. They are happy in either full sun or light shade. The golden-leaved forms ought to be

Perovskia atriplicifolia

Philadelphus 'BEAUCLERC'

Philadelphus 'VIRGINAL'

planted in light shade.

Philadelphus is often incorrectly called "Syringa", which is the Latin name for lilac and has nothing to do with philadelphus except as a result of an historical misnaming several centuries ago.

Philadelphuses do well in a large number of situations. They make good specimen plants or can be planted in groups. They are useful in an herbaceous border, where they can have their brief moment of flowering glory and then fit neatly into the background, perhaps setting off other plants, particularly those with stronger colours. The taller ones look good with late-flowering clematis climbing through them.

Propagation is from half-ripe or hardwood cuttings. Pruning should take place either after flowering or in winter, and should consist of removing some of the old and weaker wood in order to regenerate the bush.

Philadelphus 'BEAUCLERC' is one of the most popular of the hybrids. It has large white flowers with a pink flush in the middle, and grows to about 2m (6ft).

P. 'BELLE ETOILE' is another excellent form of the same height as 'BEAUCLERC'. Its single flowers have a dark pink centre and are strongly fragrant.

P. 'BURFORDENSIS' is a tall, vigorous variety, reaching a height of 3m (10ft). It has large, scentless flowers.

P. 'BURKWOODII' is a medium-sized shrub with very fragrant flowers. The white petals are stained to a rich pink toward the centre of the flower.

P. coronarius 'AUREUS' is a good golden-leaved form with single fragrant flowers. It should not be placed in full sun and is worth considering if you wish to enliven a lightly shaded corner – too much shade causes it to lose its colour and revert to green. Another form of *P. coronarius* is 'VARIEGATA' which, as its name implies, has variegated leaves edged with creamy white.

P. 'ENCHANTMENT' produces masses of fragrant double blossoms on a medium-sized (2.5m; 8ft) shrub.

P. 'MANTEAU D'HERMINE' is a dwarf form, less than a metre (3ft) high, that carries a mass of blossom.

P. microphyllus is a dense shrub of not much more than a metre (3ft) in height. The flowers are white and very fragrant.

P. 'SILVER SHOWERS' is another small shrub, reaching about a metre (3ft), with single white flowers that are very fragrant.

Philadelphus

Sp S A W
Zone 6

Philadelphus 'BELLE ETOILE'

Philadelphus 'SYBILLE'

P. 'SYBILLE' is also small and is covered in summer with very large white flowers. These have white petals that are a rose pink towards the base.

P. 'VIRGINAL' is another of the most popular varieties. This has large flowers appearing as both double and semi-double. It is a tall plant, reaching up to 3m (10ft).

There are very many more species and cultivars, differing from each other mainly in height, size of flower and degree of fragrance. The ones listed above are among the most popular and freely available, but they are all worth a try.

Phlomis

Phlomis

PHLOMIS

THIS IS ANOTHER OF those genera containing both herbaceous perennials and a number of shrubby plants that have an herbaceous appearance. The woody members are low shrubs with heavily-felted leaves and whorls of sage-like flowers stacked up the stems, almost like the layers of a wedding cake. The flowers are either yellow or pink and appear from late summer onwards. The evergreen leaves are grey green and along with the stems are clothed in fine hairs. The shrubs rarely reach more than 1.2m (4ft) high. They are quite hardy, taking frosts down to at least −14°C (7°F).

Phlomis seem to have no preference for soils, as long as they are reasonably free draining. They prefer full sun.

As these are very close to their herbaceous siblings, they can be easily accommodated in an herbaceous or mixed border, particularly as their structure is relatively open and free. They fit in well with yellow or orange schemes or with even warmer colours.

Phlomis can be propagated either from softwood cuttings or from seed. Cut back some of the old wood each year to promote new growth.

P. fruticosa, Jerusalem Sage, is the species most commonly seen. It is a loose shrub with small whorls of yellow flowers. The form 'EDWARD BOWLES' has paler flowers and larger leaves.

P. italica has lilac or pink flowers. It is not so hardy as the previous plant.

P. purpurea is also tender, with a sprawling habit and dark pink flowers.

Phlomis fruticosa

Pieris

PIERIS

THIS IS ONE OF those shrubs that leaves you uncertain whether you bought it for the flowers or the foliage. Of course, this does not matter in the least: the important thing is that you bought and are enjoying it; because enjoy it you certainly will. Great trusses of white or pink lily-of-the-valley flowers hang from the evergreen branches during the spring. They are complemented by the fiery-red growth of the young leaves, contrasting delightfully with the glossy, dark green of the older foliage. Pieris are medium-height shrubs, growing up to 4m (13ft). They are reasonably hardy, taking temperatures down to −14°C (7°F), but the young shoots can get badly burnt during late spring frosts, so they need protection from these and from cold winds.

Pieris is one of those plants that some gardeners are unable to grow, because it heartily dislikes any chalky soils. It prefers a light shady spot, preferably where it will not receive the early morning sun in spring.

The conditions of light shade and wind protection can best be achieved in a shrub border along with other bushes and trees, and pieris thrives in the company of other acid-loving plants, such as rhododendrons, perhaps with heathers around its feet. It is also

Pieris formosa forrestii 'WAKEHURST'

Pieris formosa forrestii 'WAKEHURST'

effective if planted in groups.

Propagation is from half-ripe cuttings. No pruning is required, beyond keeping the plant tidy after flowering is over, though if it has to be cut back hard it will regenerate.

Pieris 'FIRECREST' is a widely available form with red young leaves and white, scented flowers.

P. 'FOREST FLAME' gets its new growth early in spring. This growth starts as a brilliant red, fades through pink to white and then takes on the green colour of the adult leaves. It has large panicles of flowers, and is one of the finest varieties.

P. formosa forrestii is one of the best-known species. It has all the characteristics of the genus, but flowers a bit later than some of the others. It has several varieties in cultivation, the most widely-grown being 'WAKEHURST'. Like 'FOREST FLAME', of which this is one of the parents, the brilliant red leaves fade to a salmon pink before turning creamy white and then eventually dark green. It has large panicles of white flowers. Some people consider this to be the best of all the pieris, but

Pieris

S   A   W

Zone 7

it is susceptible to the late frosts.

P. japonica has long, narrow leaves that are a coppery red at their juvenile stage, and white flowers. There are several popular forms. 'BLUSH' has pink-flushed flowers, darker when in bud. 'CHRISTMAS CHEER' has dark pink flowers, tipped with a darker pink, appearing earlier than those of the species. 'PINK DELIGHT' has pale pink flowers which are darker in bud. 'PURITY' has large panicles of pure white flowers. 'VARIEGATA' is a smaller shrub with pink young leaves changing to a grey-green edged with creamy white.

P. taiwanensis is a medium-sized shrub of about 2m (6ft). The young growth is bronze and the white flower trusses are held erect.

Potentilla 'ABBOTSWOOD'

Potentilla

Potentilla

Sp (S)(A) W'

Zone 6

CINQUEFOIL

THESE WONDERFUL SMALL SHRUBS flower throughout most of the summer, lasting into autumn. Before going on to describe them, it is perhaps as well to clear up any confusion that may occur with herbaceous plants of the same name. The shrubby and the herbaceous potentillas belong to the same family and it so happens that some have woody stems and others die back in winter. The flower shape is

Potentilla 'ELIZABETH'

the same, it is only the habit that is different. It is correct to call them either potentillas or cinquefoils; if you want to distinguish them it is simplest to qualify them as either shrubby or herbaceous potentillas.

The shrubby species are small and bushy, reaching 1.25m (4ft). The flowers are flat saucers of five petals, coloured either white or shades of yellow and orange, all with a central boss of yellow. There have been attempts to produce red forms but they have not been completely successful. The leaves are small, made up of either five or three leaflets. They are deciduous but the new leaves begin to appear early in the year, and they are totally hardy.

There seems to be no restriction on the type of soil that potentillas enjoy. They are best in full sun but will tolerate a little shade.

Potentillas are marvellous plants for any garden as they are compact and flower over a long period. They fit into either a shrub or a mixed border. I find them particularly satisfying in the latter: the shape of the bush and the colour of the flowers give substance to a border. They blend or contrast attractively with a range of colours, including blues. The pale blue form of *Viola cornuta* rambling through the skirts of the potentilla creates a particularly attractive vignette.

Propagation is readily achieved from

Potentilla parvifolia

cuttings taken in early summer. No pruning is required except to remove some of the old wood. When the plant gets old, it is easiest to replace it, as potentillas grow quickly.

Potentilla arbuscula is the high-mountain equivalent of *P. fruticosa*, which means it is extremely tough. It has yellow flowers and grey-green foliage.

P. davurica has white flowers and hairy grey-green leaves. There are several cultivars but it is best in its form *P.d. mandshurica*, which is a very low-growing variety and is a good plant for shady areas. 'ABBOTSWOOD' is another good white variety, this time forming a compact bush. 'MOUNT EVEREST' is a larger bush, with large white flowers.

P. fruticosa is the parent of most of the many garden hybrids that are available. These hybrids will be considered after the list of species. *P. fruticosa* itself is a low shrub of about a metre (3ft) or less, with yellow flowers and small leaves.

P. parvifolia is a small shrub with small leaves, each composed of seven leaflets. The flowers are also on the small side and are a rich yellow colour. Again, this is the possible parent of several good forms, some of which are included below.

P. × sulphurascens is available in two pale yellow forms: 'ELIZABETH' and 'LOGAN'.

The various species and forms of Poten-

tilla have become terribly confused and many of the cultivars are being attributed to a wide variety of species. Most of the following seem to have *P. fruticosa* in them. Ultimately it does not matter where the plant comes from; what matters is whether it is worth giving it space in a garden. The following are a few of the many cultivars available. 'BEESII' (golden yellow flowers), 'DAYDAWN' (pink flowers), 'KATHERINE DYKES' (primrose flowers – one of the best cultivars), 'KLONDIKE' (large deep yellow flowers), 'MOONLIGHT' (soft yellow flowers), 'PRINCESS' (pink flowers), 'RED ACE' (red-orange flowers – not a true red but the nearest there is), 'SUNSET' (orange flowers), 'TANGERINE' (tangerine-orange flowers), and 'VILMORIANA' (cream or pale yellow flowers).

Protea

PROTEAS

THIS IS A VERY LARGE GENUS of plants, mainly from South Africa, offering a great diversity of exotic flower forms. Proteas are distinguished by cups of highly coloured bracts, each surrounding a central boss of florets. The plants themselves also vary in height and shape. The leaves are evergreen. Proteas are tender and can only be grown in the open in

Protea

Zone 10

Protea grandiceps

frost-free areas. In colder areas, the smaller shrubs can be grown in a warm conservatory or greenhouse. They make an excellent source of cut flowers.

Proteas like a well-drained soil, preferably on the acid side, with a good mulch to preserve moisture. They prefer to be in full sun.

These are such spectacular shrubs that they must be planted in positions where they can be appreciated for their beauty. The variety of colour allows a wide range of positions in mixed borders. If used as conservatory plants, they can be moved outside during the summer months.

Propagation can be achieved readily from seed. Apart from dead-heading, no pruning is required.

Protea amplexicaulis is a prostrate shrub, suitable for the large rock garden. The flowers are often borne out of sight on the underside of the branches during spring, but when seen they are a chocolate brown.

P. caffra goes to the opposite extreme, growing to a tree 4m (13ft) high. This is a summer-flowering species, with deep pink heads.

P. cynaroides, Giant Protea, is an incredible plant, with flowers measuring up to 23cm (9in) across. The bracts are of varying shades of pink. The shrub is a bit sprawling, reaching

Protea magnifica

Protea cynaroides

up to 2m (6ft) high. It flowers in late summer and autumn.

P. grandiceps, the Peach Protea, is a curious protea, with clusters of bracts that never open fully, and therefore give the appearance of deep pink-red balls. These appear throughout the summer. The shrub grows up to 2m (6ft) high and has leathery leaves with red margins.

P. longifolia has long narrow foliage, as its name implies, and greenish white flowers with touches of black. This species can flower from autumn throughout the winter. It grows up to 2m (6ft) tall.

P. magnifica offers bracts in a range of colours from white to deep pink, with floret hairs that are tipped with brown or black. This species grows up to 2m (6ft) high.

P. nana, Mountain Rose, is a low shrub of up to a metre (3ft) high, with deep pink to deep red flowers, appearing during late spring and early summer.

P. scolymocephala is covered with pale green or yellowish flowers in the autumn. They make marvellous cut flowers. This is a low shrub, growing up to a metre (3ft) high.

Prunus

ORNAMENTAL CHERRY

SPRING IS A WONDERFUL time – there are so many plants that can take your breath away; everything seems crisp and fresh, and even the air has this quality. Later, in the lazy hot days of summer, the plants usually lack this crispness, but in spring, trees covered in the foam of cherry blossom add to the feeling of marvel and well-being. I can well remember feeling very low one day a few years ago, when I happened to walk down a road lined with cherry trees in full blossom. By the time I reached the bottom of the road my spirits had lifted completely and I felt like skipping.

Common they may be, but I would rather not be without ornamental cherries. The flowers are either white or pink, and either single or double. They hang in clusters, often completely covering the tree, in early spring before the leaves appear. The leaves are ovate and, to some people, the most boring aspect of the plant, but I have always enjoyed them. There are purple-leaved varieties and some colour well in autumn.

Most people are familiar with cherries as trees, either of medium size or, sometimes, very large, but some species grow as bushes, and there are even prostrate forms. There are also weeping cherries. One disadvantage is

Prunus 'UKON'

that their roots are very wide-spreading and many have a tendency to sucker. Nearly all cherries are totally hardy, although some may experience damage to blossom due to late frosts. *Prunus* is a very large genus, because although I have been referring to cherries, it also includes the almonds, apricots, peaches and plums.

There seems to be no problem over the choice of soils. They generally prefer a sunny position but will tolerate a little light shade.

These are specimen trees to grow by themselves in a lawn or against other trees, preferably trees already in foliage, so that they will show off the blossom at its best. The white form looks good against a blue sky and can be enchanting in the spring twilight. Cherries are not generally recommended for the herbaceous border because of their habit of suckering, but some of the shrubby forms are excellent in a mixed border.

Cherries are usually propagated by grafting suitable material onto the stock of *Prunus avium*. No pruning is required.

Prunus 'ACCOLADE' is an early-flowering variety with good clusters of large pink flowers.

Prunus

Sp S A W
Zone 6

Prunus 'AMANOGAWA'

Prunus 'KIKU-SHIDARE SAKURA'

P. 'AMANOGAWA' has a very upright, columnar stance. The flowers are pink, semi-double and fragrant.

P. *avium*, Gean, is the wild cherry that is native to Europe. It has single white flowers and can grow very large. The small fruit is popular with birds, who scatter the seed, from which arise seedlings. This cherry is liable to sucker if the roots are damaged. There is a double form 'PLENA' (or sometimes 'FLORE PLENO').

P. × *blireiana* is one of the plums, with purple leaves and masses of double, pink flowers.

P. *cerasifera*, Cherry Plum, is a white-flowered species, though it is best known in its form 'NIGRA', which has single pink flowers and dark purple foliage. 'PISSARDII' also has pink flowers and purple leaves, but in both cases not quite so dark as 'NIGRA'.

P. × *cistena* is another form with dark foliage. This time it is a shrub, reaching no more than 2m (6ft) high. It has white flowers and should be pruned after flowering.

P. *dulcis*, Almond, has pink or white flowers borne very early in spring. In fact, it is one of the earliest to flower. Although it occasionally bears fruit, it is mainly grown for its blossom.

P. *glandulosa* is a small shrub cherry, growing up to 1.5m (5ft) high. It has white or pink flowers. There are two double forms, of which 'ALBAPLENA' is white and 'ROSEA PLENA' (or 'SINENSIS') is pink.

P. 'KANZAN' is one of the commonest of the double cherries. Its masses of darker pink flowers can be a sorry sight in a wet season. Much despised of late because of the unsubtle colour of the flowers and its boring shape for the rest of the year, it can still be a lovely sight in a good year. The leaves have a rich autumn coloration.

P. 'KIKU-SHIDARE SAKURA', Cheal's Weeping Cherry, is a small weeping tree with double, bright pink flowers.

P. *padus*, Bird Cherry, can grow into quite a large tree. Its small white flowers are fragrant. There are several varieties available: 'COLORATA' has pink flowers, with leaves that are purplish when young, while 'WATERERI' has long racemes of white flowers, looking almost like a buddleia in appearance.

P. 'PANDORA' is an early spring form with pale pink flowers.

P. *sargentii*, Sargent Cherry, has single pale pink flowers. The tree can reach very large proportions and can look very stately. It has brilliant autumn colouring. There are a number of cultivars, of which 'RANCHO' is the most common. This has flowers of a deeper colour than the species.

P. *serrulata* has large, white, double

Prunus tenella 'FIRE HILL'

flowers. It has quite a number of varieties including 'PINK PERFECTION', which has pink flowers. Some of the varieties with Japanese names have *P. serrulata* blood in them.

P. 'SHIROFUGEN' has bronze leaves when young. It has white flowers that are pink in bud and then finally age to pink again.

P. 'SHIROTAE' has white, semi-double flowers appearing early. They are scented.

P. subhirtella 'AUTUMNALIS' is a wonderful plant – it starts to put out its white flowers in late autumn and continues right through the winter into spring. This is not a spectacular display of masses of flower, but just a steady stream of blossom that gives a great deal of pleasure during the winter months. Frost may

Prunus 'KANZAN'

Prunus 'SHIROTAE'

kill off some of the flowers but the tree soon recovers. The form 'AUTUMNALIS ROSEA' has pink flowers, and there are several weeping forms available.

P. 'TAI HAKU', Great White Cherry, has large pure white flowers. The young foliage is bronzy.

P. tenella is a wonderful shrubby cherry, that rises to 1.2m (4ft). Upright branches are clothed in bright rose-pink flowers, just as the leaves are breaking. There is a good form, 'FIRE HILL', that has darker flowers. Increase by layering and prune after flowering.

P. triloba is another shrubby cherry, and makes a bigger plant than the previous species. The wild form has single white or pale pink

flowers, but the common form in cultivation has pink, double flowers, with petals that are arranged like a rosette. The main cultivar, 'MULTIPLEX', has pink, double flowers.

P. 'UKON' has pale greenish-white, semi-double flowers.

P × *yedoensis* has white or pink flowers. It is a spreading tree and is grown mainly in its weeping forms, such as 'IVENSII' or 'SHIDARE YOSHINO'.

Rhododendron

RHODODENDRON

APART FROM ROSES, THIS must be one of the largest genera of flowering plants in cultivation. This is surprising, since many people are denied the opportunity of growing rhododendrons because of their absolute hatred of chalky soils. There must be some charismatic quality that makes people want to specialize in these particular plants and, indeed, to breed them, for many of the cultivars are the work of amateurs. Although rhododendrons have many superlative qualities, this is hard to understand, but perhaps it is due in part to the enormous variety within the genus.

Starting with size, rhododendrons range from dwarf species grown in pots up to vast

Rhododendron

Zone 7

Rhododendron arboreum (white form)

trees, best seen from across a valley. Whether the tree is small or large, it can be completely covered in blooms. The flowers themselves can vary considerably in size. They are basically either a trumpet or a bell shape, held together in terminal clusters. With the exceptions of a true blue and black, all the colours are represented, both individually or in combinations. Apart from some of the azaleas, rhododendrons are evergreen. The leaves are generally ovate, glossy and dark green. Some have felting on the back, often of a brown or grey colour. Some are tender but there are plenty that are completely hardy, so this does not matter.

The genus includes the plants that are normally referred to as azaleas, but the difference between a rhododendron and an azalea is far from easy to describe. Strictly speaking, there is no such thing as an azalea. Originally azaleas were given a genus of their own; later, they were incorporated into the classification of rhododendrons, where there was a section called 'AZALEA', which included a lot of the varieties that we loosely call azaleas. In more recent classifications, however, this section has been eliminated and its members split between other sections, none of which bear the now-defunct name of 'AZALEA'. So azaleas have ceased to exist.

Where does that leave us? Azaleas as such no longer exist, but there is an obvious group, with blurred edges, that are sold and generally recognized as such and undoubtedly this will continue. Since some readers will be interested, I ought not to duck the issue and will list some of the characteristics that separated azaleas from rhododendrons. It was considered that rhododendrons have ten stamens and azaleas have less, often five. This is generally true but far from foolproof, as both are variable. Azaleas are elepidote (they do not have scales); the hairs on the leaves and elsewhere are unbranched; the ovaries are invariably five-celled, and the seeds are never tailed, all of which is scarcely informative to the average gardener.

Rhododendrons must have acid or neutral soil. They dislike even a hint of lime, even in the water. On the whole they all prefer light shade, although some will take a fair amount of sun.

An informal woodland setting is the ideal place for rhododendrons, particularly if it can be arranged that the wood is on the side of a valley. Few of us are fortunate enough to have such grounds so a compromise is called for: in practice, rhododendrons can look very attractive mixed in with other trees and shrubs on the margins of a garden or in a shrub border. When in flower, they make magnificent specimen bushes. It is difficult to fit them into

Rhododendron luteum

Rhododendron 'AVALANCHE'

an herbaceous border setting, and association with other plants is always a problem, but I feel they look best with other acid lovers such as camellias, pieris or the heathers.

Propagation is from seed (except for named varieties), summer cuttings, layering and grafting. Pruning is not required except, possibly, to reduce the size of the plant. This can be achieved by cutting back heavily in winter, in which case the plant usually responds and will regenerate. Some people consider that dead-heading is important to the vitality of the plant. This should be done carefully so as not to damage the new emerging buds.

The list of species and cultivars is vast, running into thousands and in no way is it possible to list them all. What follows is a list of *some* of the more worthy and easily obtainable varieties. It is in three sections: rhododendron species, hybrids, and then, perpetuating the old division, azaleas.

Rhododendron arboreum is, as its name suggests, a tree rhododendron. Its only cultivars have flowers of white, pink and red. It flowers early.

R. augustinii is a medium-sized shrub, up to 5m (16ft) high, with small leaves. The flowers range from lavender to purple and a number of cultivars is available.

R. campylocarpum is a medium-sized shrub, growing up to 3m (10ft) high, but often much smaller and compact. It has yellow, bell-shaped flowers. There are many cultivars.

R. cinnabarinum is the same stature as the previous plant, but has red or orange-red, trumpet-shaped flowers. Again many forms are available.

R. ferrugineum, the Alpine Rose, is a native of the European Alps. It is a small species, growing to only a metre (3ft) or slightly more. It has tubular flowers that are deep rose in colour.

R. keiskei is a dwarf up to 60cm (2ft), with yellow bell-shaped flowers. 'YAKU FAIRY' is a marvellous form with creamy yellow flowers.

R. luteum is a well-known yellow azalea with very fragrant flowers. It is deciduous.

R. ponticum is native to Spain, Portugal and Asia Minor and has naturalized in many parts of the world. It has mauve flowers and can be used for a large screen or windbreak.

R. maximum, a pinkish purple with yellowish dots, is not frequently grown, but has given rise to many hybrids, some of which are listed below.

R. thompsonii is a taller species up to 6m (20ft). It has blood-red, trumpet-shaped flowers.

R. wardii is half the height of the previous plant. It has bright yellow flowers that are more open than most, almost saucer-shaped.

R. williamsianum is a relatively dwarf

Rhododendron arboreum (pink form)

form, reaching 1.2m (4ft). It has shell-pink flowers and the young leaves are bronze in colour and fairly small.

R. yakushimanum is one of the best rhododendrons. Again it is only about 1.2m (4ft) high. It has white flowers flushed with pink, opening from pink buds, and several forms are available.

The following list includes only a selection from the vast number of rhododendron hybrids:

'ALISON JOHNSTONE' (yellow, flushed with pink), 'AVALANCHE' (white with a rose basal blotch and fragrant), 'BADEN BADEN' (scarlet), 'BETTY WORMALD' (dark pink with red speckling), 'BLUE PETER' (lavender blue), 'BOW BELLS' (pink with red speckles), 'BRITANNIA' (scarlet), 'CHINK' (primrose with greenish speckling), 'CHRISTMAS CHEER' (blush pink, darker in bud and early flowering), 'COWSLIP' (cream with pink blush and pink in bud), 'CURLEW' (yellow with lovat markings), 'CYNTHIA' (rose pink with crimson spotting), 'DONCASTER' (dark red), 'ELIZABETH HOBBIE' (deep red), 'FASTUOSUM FLORE PLENO' (double mauve), 'GOMER WATERER' (white,

Rhododendron yakushimanum

tinged with mauve and with a yellow-brown basal blotch), 'HUMMING BIRD' (carmine pink), 'KLUIS SENSATION' (scarlet with darker spots), 'LADY CHAMBERLAIN' (orange and red), 'LADY CLEMENTINE MITFORD' (peach pink, fading to blushed white in the centre), 'LODER'S WHITE' (pure white from pink buds), 'MAY DAY' (scarlet), 'MRS G.W. LEAK' (pink with darker spots), 'PRINCESS ANNE' (yellow with green markings), 'PTARMIGAN' (white), 'PURPLE SPLENDOUR' (deep purple, with darker markings), 'SAPPHIRE' (pale blue), 'SAPPHO' (mauve in bud, opening to white with a deep purple blotch), 'SONGBIRD' (deep violet), 'TREWITHEN ORANGE' (orange tinged with pink) and 'WINSOME' (pink).

The following are generally sold as azaleas: 'AMOENA' (double purple), 'BLUE DANUBE' (rich purple), 'CECILE' (salmon pink with a yellow flare), 'FAVORITE' (rose pink), 'GIBRALTAR' (orange red with a yellow flare), 'HINAMAYO' (pink), 'HINO CRIMSON' (bright crimson), 'HINODEGIRI' (bright red), 'HOMEBUSH' (deep pink double), 'JOHN CAIRNS' (orange red), 'MOTHER'S DAY' (double crimson), 'ORANGE BEAUTY' (orange), 'PERSIL' (white with a yellow flare), 'PURPLE TRIUMPH' (purple), 'SILVER SLIPPER' (white with a yellow flare), and 'VUYK'S ROSY RED' (a deep, rosy red).

Rhododendron thompsonii

Ribes

FLOWERING CURRANT

Ribes

Zone 6

ONE OF THE EARLIEST spring shrubs to burst into leaf and flower, particularly if in a warm spot, is *Ribes sanguineum*, with its tassels of pink flowers and the rather pungent smell that is not to everybody's taste. There are other flowering currants, with similar tassels but in yellow and white. The bushes grow up to about 2.1m (7ft) high and the leaves are the typical three-lobed leaves of the currant. The shrub is totally hardy.

Flowering currants are found growing on most soils. Full sun or light shade are tolerated, although the former is probably best.

This shrub is pretty during its flowering season, but is not much to look at for the rest of the year and is therefore best placed towards the back of a border, where the flowers can be seen in spring, but the shrub is partially covered up by later-flowering plants. One way to improve its appearance is to run a late-flowering clematis through it. Some people find the musty smell of the leaves offensive, which is another reason for planting it a little way back from a path.

Flowering currants are easily propagated from cuttings at any time. Some of the old wood should be taken out each year to stimulate new growth.

Ribes americanum has racemes of yellow flowers and its leaves offer very good autumn colour, turning from green to yellow with an orange flush.

R. × gordonianum has tassels that are coppery red on the outside and yellow inside.

R. laurifolium is an attractive form with greenish white flowers and evergreen elliptic leaves with red veining. It flowers in late winter and is comparatively small, reaching about a metre (3ft).

R. odoratum has rich yellow flowers with the scent of cloves. Its berries are edible.

R. sanguineum has rose-pink flowers and is the most common species. There are quite a number of forms with differing shades of pink. 'ALBUM' has pinkish white flowers. 'ATRORUBENS' has blood-red flowers. 'BROCKLE-

Ribes laurifolium

BANKII' has pink flowers and rich yellow leaves. It needs partial shade. 'KING EDWARD VII' has deep crimson flowers and is usually reckoned to be the best form. 'PULBOROUGH SCARLET' has deep red flowers and is also very popular. 'SPLENDENS' has deep crimson flowers. 'TYDEMAN'S WHITE' is the best of the white-flowered forms.

R. *speciosum* is like a gooseberry shrub, with typical gooseberry leaves and thorns. The flowers are red and look like small fuchsias. This is an intriguing bush but unfortunately it is slightly tender and may need wall protection in colder areas.

reasonably hardy, taking frosts down to at least −12°C (10°F), and they are also very tolerant of air pollution, making them an ideal tree to plant in town gardens (as long as these are big enough). The one drawback to robinias is that they are a bit brittle, so they have to be sheltered from strong winds; again, a town environment is ideal.

They are not at all fussy about the soil, as long as it is not too rich. They prefer full sun but will take a light shade.

Robinia is a specimen tree, growing too large to fit into a border or shrubbery. It looks good against a blue sky or against a group of trees with darker foliage.

Propagation is from seed or grafting. No pruning is required except to tidy up any broken branches.

Robinia hispida is one of the smaller species (2.5m; 8ft) and is really a shrub. It has pendulous racemes of rose-pink flowers. It suckers a lot and has vicious bristles or thorns. Fortunately the form 'MACROPHYLLA' is almost thornless. This also has large trusses of flowers.

R. *kelseyi* is another species that is not quite certain whether it is a shrub or a tree. It is slightly taller than the previous species but

Robinia hispida

Robinia

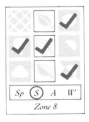

Sp (S) A W
Zone 8

Robinia

FALSE ACACIA

THESE TREES ALWAYS MANAGE to look fresh and cool, creating an impression of lightness and movement. It is the light green, pinnate leaves that give them this quality, which they retain even when they reach their full height. It is not only the leaves that make this a desirable tree; the flowers also have an attractive appeal. They belong to the pea family and hang in long trusses, or racemes, in early summer. The colour varies from white to pink. The trees are

Robinia pseudacacia

retains the same sharp bristles. The flowers are again deep pink.

R. pseudacacia has large hanging clusters of white, fragrant flowers. This will eventually make a very big tree and will need plenty of room, but it needs protection from the wind. Several forms are available, of which 'FRISIA' is the best. This has very pale yellowish green leaves that turn yellow in autumn. It is a marvellous plant for a darkish corner as long as it is not in too full shade.

Romneya

TREE POPPY; CALIFORNIAN TREE POPPY

THIS IS A VERY attractive Californian shrub. Its glistening white, tissue-paper flowers have an enormous boss of golden stamens at the centre. The flowers are up to 15cm (6in) across and are sweetly fragrant. They continue to appear throughout summer and well into autumn, and are nicely set off by blue-green leaves. The shrub grows to about 2m (6ft) and mildly suckers around making a dense clump. Tree poppies are fairly tough and will survive most winters, down to at least −15°C (4°F). They are by nature semi-

herbaceous and may die back to ground level.

They prefer lighter, free-draining soils and also like full sun.

These really are beautiful plants, fitting perfectly into a wide range of herbaceous and mixed borders. A green background shows them up to good advantage. The white flowers enable them to mix well with many different planting schemes, although their size and their long flowering season keeps them as a constant focus of attention.

They can be propagated from rooted suckers. All branches and shoots should be pruned back to just above ground level after flowering.

Romneya coulteri is the main species and has been described above. It is by far the commonest available.

R.× hybrida is the result of a cross between the species above and the one below. One of the resulting forms, 'WHITE CLOUD', is supposed to be superior. This has large, fragrant flowers.

R. trichocalyx is very closely related to *R. coulteri*. Its leaves are more finely cut, the stems are more slender, and the calyx is covered with bristles, but all these points are minor: visually it is very similar to *R. coulteri*.

Romneya

Sp (S) (A) *W*

Zone 7

Romneya coulteri

Rosa

Zone 7

Rosa

ROSE

ROSES MUST BE THE most frequently grown of all the flowering plants in our gardens, and this has been so throughout history. Much has been written over the centuries by poets and others, extolling the virtues of the rose, and it would be invidious of me to try and match their eloquence or sensitivity. Suffice it to say that virtually everybody likes the rose.

Individually there are so many varieties that it is difficult to know where to start. The colour range is very extensive, although the elusive blue still eludes the hybridizers. The size of the blooms and plants is equally variable, as is the scent. The classification of roses, while not as complicated as that of rhododendrons, leads to confusion, partly because there have been changes in recent years. The formal classification need not worry us here, but hybrid teas and floribundas have officially ceased to exist: the former mainly fall into a group called "large flowered roses" and the latter "cluster roses". Change comes slowly to such areas as rose growing, however, and because the old terms are still very much in use they will be retained here.

Newcomers to rose-growing may find the range on offer totally bewildering, so it is perhaps a good idea to look at the different

Rosa (hybrid tea) 'ENA HARKNESS'

types of roses and their uses. The hybrid teas (large-flowered roses) and floribundas (cluster roses) have traditionally been used for bedding purposes and are usually pruned heavily each year. They often have repeated or continuous flowering throughout the summer. The plants are usually stiff and rather formal. Hybrid teas have a single bloom per stem, whereas the floribundas have several.

All roses are shrubs, but the term "shrub rose" has been used for those roses that are grown in a more informal manner. They are bred as free-ranging bushes rather than a few

Rosa (floribunda) 'PINK PARFAIT'

Rosa (hybrid tea) 'FRAGRANT CLOUD'

stems whose function is simply to support the roses. Shrub roses are traditionally used as specimen bushes or as part of a mixed border. (Increasingly, however, hybrid teas and floribundas are also being used in the latter situation.) Shrub roses contain all the so-called "old-fashioned" roses; those created in the current century are referred to as "modern shrub roses". The old-fashioned shrub roses are generally subdivided into further categories – gallica, centifolia, alba, bourbon, moss and damask – according to their parentage and characteristics.

Climbers and ramblers both shoot heavenwards with very long, arching stems. The distinction between the two is not all that

Rosa (shrub) 'FANTIN-LATOUR'

they will never do well. If you want to replant in the same place, change the soil in that area. To get the best out of a rose it should be planted in full sun, although some light shade, on the north side of a house for example, will be tolerated. Most roses are reasonably hardy.

In common with a growing number of people, my own preference is to associate roses with other plants, so that it is possible to get a better blend of textures and colours. In a bed containing nothing but roses, the repetitive nature of the plants and similarity of

Rosa (climber) 'KIFTSGATE'

Rosa (shrub) 'CANARY BIRD'

evident and is not too important here. Ramblers generally ramble and climbers climb. Amplifying this slightly, ramblers are ideal for covering sheds, banks, fences or pergolas and tend to be the equivalent of the shrub roses, both in their long history and in that they only flower once a year. Climbers are more closely related to the hybrid teas and often flower continuously or at least fitfully throughout the summer. They can be used for the same purposes as ramblers, as well as on walls. Both need tying to supports.

Roses seem to flourish on most soils, though they undoubtedly prefer rich, fertile soils. Do not plant roses in the same soil from which you have just removed other roses;

Rosa (rambler) 'DOROTHY PERKINS'

flower shape, and often colour, detracts from the quality and beauty of the individual plant. It is not enough to underplant a bed of roses with a few bulbs or make a token planting of pinks round the edge of the border: this only seems to make the matter worse. Roses should be placed in mixed and herbaceous borders where their colour and structure will complement other plants. Here, they can be used not only to improve the overall appearance of the border, but to set up attractive contrasts, so that each plant is brought into focus and stands on its own merit.

Propagation is from cuttings or grafting. The species roses can be propagated from seed. Pruning is a complex business as there are so many types to consider. For a start all dead, damaged or frosted wood should be removed. For hybrid teas, hard pruning is frequently practised, all stems being cut back to the first pair of sound buds. Other people prefer lighter pruning for these as well as for floribundas. Here the older wood should be removed at the end of winter, in order to promote new growth, and newer wood should be shortened by a third. Shrub roses should have the older material removed, again to

promote new growth. Climbers need little attention beyond keeping the plant tidy and possibly dead-heading. Ramblers should have some of the old growth removed immediately after flowering.

There are so many roses that it is very difficult to know what to recommend in such a small space. Many books are devoted entirely to roses, and the reader is urged to consult these if he is really becoming a rose addict. With so many similar varieties it is very difficult to distinguish between them with the written word and by far the best course is to go and look at the roses in flower in nurseries or rose gardens. The following is just a brief list, giving little more than the colour of some of the more popular varieties.

Shrub roses: 'AGNES' (deep yellow rugosa), 'BALLERINA' (pink modern with white centre), 'CANARY BIRD' (small bright yellow modern, very early flowering), 'CONSTANCE SPRY' (rose-pink modern), 'DUNWICH ROSE' (soft creamy yellow modern, early flowering), 'EMPRESS JOSEPHINE' (semi-double, heavily-veined, rose-pink gallica), 'FANTIN-LATOUR' (pale pink centifolia), 'FÉLICITÉ PARMENTIER' (soft salmon-pink alba), 'FRAU DAGMAR HARTROPP' or 'HASTRUP' (pink rugosa), 'FRED LOADS' (vermilion modern), 'FRÜHLINGS-GOLD' (yellow modern), 'FRÜHLINGSMORGEN', (pink modern with yellow centre), 'GOLDEN

Rosa (shrub) 'FRAU DAGMAR HARTOPP'

WINGS' (soft yellow modern with red stamens), 'HAMBURG' (crimson modern), 'HENRI MARTIN' (semi-double crimson moss), 'KATHLEEN HARROP' (shell pink bourbon), 'LAFTER' (salmon rose modern) 'MME ISAAC PEREIRE' (deep pink bourbon), 'MAGENTA' (lilac-pink to mauve modern), 'NEVADA' (creamy white modern), 'NUITS DE YOUNG' (maroon-purple moss), 'OMAR KHAYYAM' (pink damask), 'PETITE DE HOLLANDE' (double pink centifolia), 'ROBERT LE DIABLE' (crimson centifolia), 'ROSA MUNDI' (pale pink, striped crimson gallica), 'SISSINGHURST CASTLE' (purplish crimson gallica), 'TUSCANY' (crimson gallica), and 'WILHELM' (crimson modern).

Climbers: 'COPENHAGEN' (scarlet), 'GOLDEN SHOWERS' (yellow), 'ICEBERG' (white), 'KIFTSGATE' (creamy white), 'MAIGOLD' (yellow), 'NEW DAWN' (pink), 'PINK PERPETUÉ' (deep pink), 'PURITY' (white), and 'ZÉPHIRINE DROUHIN' (cerise pink, semi-double).

Ramblers: 'ALBÉRIC BARBIER' (creamy white), 'ALBERTINE' (coppery pink), 'DOROTHY PERKINS' (pink), 'FÉLICITÉ ET PERPETUÉ (creamy white), and 'RAMBLING RECTOR' (double white).

Hybrid Teas: 'ALEC'S RED' (cherry red), 'BLESSINGS' (coral pink), 'BONSOIR' (peach), 'CARLA' (pink), 'CHRISTIAN DIOR' (scarlet), 'DOREEN' (orange yellow), 'ELLEN WILMOTT' (cream and pink), 'ENA HARKNESS' (crimson),

Rosa (climber) 'ZÉPHIRINE DROUHIN'

'FIRST LOVE' (rose pink), 'FRAGRANT CLOUD' (red), 'GRANDPA DICKSON' (yellow), 'HARRY WHEATCROFT' (orange and yellow), 'NORMAN HARTNELL' (crimson), 'PEACE' (yellow and pink), 'PINK FAVOURITE' (pink), 'SHOT SILK' (salmon pink), 'SILVER JUBILEE' (silver pink), 'SUTTER'S GOLD' (orange yellow) and 'WENDY CUSSONS' (scarlet).

Floribundas: 'AMA' (scarlet), 'ANNE COCKER' (vermilion), 'CHANELLE' (creamy pink), 'CHORUS GIRL' (vermilion), 'ELIZABETH OF GLAMIS' (salmon), 'ICEBERG' (white), 'KIM' (yellow), 'LILI MARLENE' (red), 'ORANGE SENSATION' (bright orange), 'PINK PARFAIT' (varying shades of pink), 'RED DANDY' (scarlet), and 'ZAMBRA' (tangerine).

Rosa (floribunda) 'ICEBERG'

Rosmarinus

ROSEMARY

THIS IS A VERY SMALL GENUS of which only one species is in general cultivation and has been for many centuries. This is mainly because it is a much-valued herb, but in addition to its culinary and herbal qualities rosemary is an

Rosmarinus

Sp (S) (A) W
Zone 7

on the leaves. 'BENENDEN BLUE' is the best of the forms, with vivid blue flowers. 'MAJORCA PINK' has lilac-pink flowers. 'MISS JESSUP'S UPRIGHT', as its name suggests, is a very upright, columnar plant. *R.o. roseus* has pink flowers. 'SEVEN SEAS' is a very popular free-flowering form, but it is slightly tender and requires wall protection in colder areas.

Rubus

BRAMBLE

BRAMBLES NEED NOT DETAIN us long as, although there are quite a few ornamental ones, including several with fine stems, there are only three that are worth growing for their flowers alone. They form medium-sized loose bushes with arching stems. In spite of being brambles, two are completely without prickles but the third, alas, has these. The flowers are white or pink, with a yellow central boss of stamens, and they can measure up to 5cm (2in) across. The leaves are trifoliate and soft to the touch. The shrubs grow up to about 2m (10ft) and are hardy.

Brambles do not seem to have any particular soil requirements. Light shade is preferred, but they will also thrive in full sun.

These are often neglected as shrubs, but

Rubus × tridel

Rubus

Sp (S) A W
Zone 6

Rosmarinus officinalis

attractive bush. The flowers are a violet blue, set against narrow linear leaves of a gentle grey green. The whole has a fine fragrance. It is fairly hardy, taking winters down to at least −14°C (7°F), though it appreciates a little protection from a wall, particularly against cold winds.

Rosemary is not fussy about soils as long as they are free draining. It prefers full sun, but will take a little bit of light shade.

This lovely plant fits into a wide variety of situations, including shrub and mixed borders. It is a good shrub to position near a path that is frequently used, as it is a joy to run one's hands through it in passing. Use in the kitchen is another reason for keeping it near a path, where its soft colours will allow it to blend well with many other plants.

Rosemary can be propagated easily from summer cuttings. Pruning is not necessary; indeed, it can ruin the bush as it is loath to break again from old wood.

Rosmarinus officinalis is the species in general cultivation but a number of cultivars are available. *R.o. alba* has white flowers. *R.o. angustissimus* is very narrow leaved and a deep blue colour. *R.o. aureus* has golden variegations they are delightful to look at and have a long flowering season. Shrubberies or mixed borders are the best location for them. They are a bit on the large side for a mainly herbaceous border, but there is no problem with colour schemes if you want to include a bramble. They also make fine specimen plants.

Propagation is from half-ripe cuttings. Pruning takes the form of removing some of the older wood each year and is essential if the shrub is to keep a constant supply of new growth.

Rubus odoratus has purple-pink flowers on thornless stems. The flowers are fragrant.

R. spectabilis, Salmonberry, is slightly shorter in stature. The flowers are purplish red and scented. This is the one with the prickles.

R. × tridel has large white flowers. It has a very fine form, 'BENENDEN', with bigger flowers. Both can be a stunning sight.

Santolina chamaecyparissus

Santolina

COTTON LAVENDER

THE COTTON LAVENDERS ARE mainly thought of as foliage plants but there is one, *S. rosmarinifolia*, that is also a fine flowering plant. Cotton lavenders are really sub-shrubs, halfway between hardy perennials and shrubs. They are fairly small, not reaching above 60cm (2ft), and form a dome of foliage from which the yellow flowers appear on long stalks. They are reasonably hardy, taking temperatures down to −12°C (10°F).

They will tolerate any kind of soil, but it must be free draining. Full sun is also a necessary requirement.

These are perfect for the herbaceous and mixed borders, but they are also attractive plants for a large rock garden or a bank. Alternatively, they can be used to form low compact hedges along paths.

Propagation is from summer cuttings. Pruning is restricted to a light trimming in spring to keep them neat and compact.

Santolina chamaecyparissus has excellent silver foliage and insignificant yellow flowers.

The silver foliage fits in with many colour schemes, but the flowers may clash, so they are often removed. They will, however, fit into yellow schemes.

S. pinnata is a larger and more lax version of the previous plant.

S. rosmarinifolia forms a bright green hummock of foliage with bright yellow flowers like buttons, held above it on thin stems. The whole thing has an air of complete freshness. If grown well, in a wind-free spot, the hummock is hemispherical and the flowers describe a parallel surface above it – a marvellous sight. There is one slight problem and that is that the bright, almost citrus, yellow is difficult to combine with other colours. It needs careful placing, but is well worth the effort.

Santolina

Sp (*S*) *A* *W*
Zone 7

Sarcococca

CHRISTMAS BOX

IN MANY WAYS these are insignificant shrubs, but their small white flowers have a very sweet fragrance during the winter months. Another point in their favour is that they will grow in

Sarcococca

Sp *S* *A* (*W*)
Zone 6

quite deep shade. They have shiny green evergreen leaves that clothe the erect stems. Sarcococca suckers around quite freely forming a dense bush that can reach up to 2m (6ft) in height and width. There seems to be no problem with hardiness.

This plant will tolerate any soil, including chalk, and will put up with anything from full sun to quite deep shade.

The best way to use sarcococca is to tuck it in a place where it can be enjoyed during the winter months. It will grow happily under taller shrubs or trees, as long as the soil is not too impoverished. It is a good plant to grow for use in winter flower arrangements, although some people might find its all-pervading fragrance a bit too sickly.

Sarcococca can easily be propagated from rooted suckers. No pruning is required.

The different species are so similar in appearance that it seems pointless to repeat the same information under each one. The following are the main species that are available: *Sarcococca confusa*; *S. hookeriana*, particularly in its variety 'DIGYNA'; *S. humilis* and *S. ruscifolia*.

Senecio

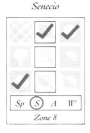

	✓	✓
✓		

Sp (S) A W
Zone 8

Senecio laxifolius

Senecio

SHRUBBY RAGWORT

THIS IS AN EXTREMELY large genus, containing several useful shrubby plants with silver foliage and yellow or white daisy-like flowers. The bushes reach about 2m (6ft) in height and can become rather lax. The evergreen foliage is silver green in colour, the silver being particularly intense on the reverse and around the margins. The flowering period is relatively short, in the first half of summer. In some forms the flowers are a very bright golden yellow, in others they are rather dull and gardeners often remove the flowering stems and use the plant entirely as a foliage plant. They all come from New Zealand and so are not completely hardy in colder areas. In free-draining soil and a sunny position, most will survive an average winter as long as the temperature does not drop much below $-10°$ to $-12°$C ($14°$ to $10°$F). They are, however, wind and salt tolerant, making them very useful seaside shrubs.

They are not fussy about the soil as long as it is free draining. They definitely prefer full sun, looking very sulky in shade.

Shrubby ragworts are very valuable as foliage plants and their silver quality can be used in a variety of areas, including shrub, mixed and even herbaceous borders. The

Sarcococca hookeriana 'DIGYNA'

Senecio greyi

S. 'SUNSHINE' is by far the best of the bunch in all respects. It has good foliage, masses of bright yellow flowers, with a longer season than most, and it is hardier.

Solanum

Solanum

Sp Ⓢ Ⓐ *W*
Zone 8

SOLANUM

THIS IS A VERY LARGE genus that includes potatoes, tomatoes and deadly nightshade. It is an extremely diverse group of plants, including two very good flowering climbers that ought to have a space found for them. They are both on the tender side, but if grown against a wall they should survive most winters: they might be cut back but will quickly regenerate without apparent loss of flowering ability. They both have potato-like flowers; in one species these are white and in the other, blue. The flowering is profuse and continues from spring to late autumn. If supported, these delightful and rewarding climbers will grow to more than 6m (20ft).

They seem to thrive on any soil as long as it is free draining. Both species like full sun.

Both can be grown up a wall or trellis and are a spectacle in their own right with a long flowering period. Propagation is from sum-

Solanum crispum 'GLASNEVIN'

intense yellow flowers of some varieties restrict their placement in certain colour schemes, but this is no excuse to ignore the plant or remove its flowers. It is a reason for giving it careful consideration so that it can be enjoyed at its best.

Propagation is from summer cuttings. Pruning is necessary every few years to keep the bushes from getting too lax. This should be undertaken immediately after flowering and you can cut back into old wood. If flowers are not required, the plant can be sheared over every spring before flowering.

Senecio bicolor cineraria is a rather tender sub-shrub that is used as a bedding plant. It has very good felted silver foliage, but has little importance as a flowering shrub.

S. compactus is another plant on the tender side. It has very attractive white leaves with wavy edges. The flowers are bright yellow.

S. greyi is a very good plant with fine yellow flowers. It is very close to both *S. laxifolius* and *S.* 'SUNSHINE', with which it is often confused.

S. laxifolius is often confused with other plants as mentioned above, but a few nurseries are offering the true plant. It is not very hardy.

S. reinoldii is a much taller plant, growing up to 6m (20ft) or more. It makes a good shelter belt near the sea, but the flowers have an unpleasant scent.

Solanum jasminoides 'ALBUM'

mer cuttings. The only pruning is to keep the plants tidy and to remove any frosted wood.

Solanum crispum is the blue-flowered climber. This is mainly known in its form 'GLASNEVIN', which is a superb plant with a very extended flowering period. It has even flowered in winter in my garden between two periods of frost that went down to −10°C (14°F) followed by −14°C (7°F). 'GLASNEVIN' looks attractive with *Clematis viticella* 'ROYAL VELOURS' growing through it.

Solanum jasminoides is less vigorous and is usually grown in its form 'ALBUM', which has pure white flowers. This is slightly more tender than the previous species, but it is a truly beautiful plant.

hardy and is an excellent shrub for coastal regions as it will stand wind and salt.

It is not at all fussy about the type of soil it inhabits as long as this is free draining. It prefers full sun but will tolerate light shade.

This is a big loose shrub that does well either in a shrub border or on a boundary, though it is too coarse for the mixed or herbaceous border.

Propagation is from seed or from summer cuttings. No pruning is required. It does not break easily from old wood.

Not only is there only one species in this genus, but there also appear to be no varieties or cultivars. Here is a plant that keeps itself very much to itself.

Spartium junceum

Spiraea

SPIRAEA

THIS IS QUITE A LARGE GENUS of flowering shrubs, split into two types: those that flower in the late spring and those that do so much later in the year. In general, the early flowerers are white and the later ones pink or red. The individual flowers are small but they are made up into large, flat-headed panicles, or long racemes. The leaves vary in size but are never very big, generally being elliptic or ovate in shape. The height of the bushes is rarely above 2m (6ft), often much less. Spiraeas are extremely hardy and should have no problems surviving the winter.

Spartium

Sp (S) A W
Zone 6

Spartium

SPANISH BROOM

THIS IS ANOTHER of the brooms, in this case growing to a very tall bush up to 4m (13ft) high. It is a monotypic genus, its only member being *S. junceum*. This has very little foliage and that which is present is narrow and the same dark green as the stems. The blossom takes the form of typical, pea-like, broom flowers. These are bright yellow and comparatively large. Spanish broom is reasonably

Spiraea 'ARGUTA'

Spiraea

Zone 8

Any soil is likely to provide a good home for these plants. They much prefer full sun but will take some light shade.

These are pretty shrubs that can be treated in a number of ways. They are effective in mass plantings in a shrub border or as single plants in a mixed or even herbaceous border. Some of the early-flowering types give colour and structure to the herbaceous border before other plants have got under way. Some are suitable for making informal hedges.

Spiraea can be propagated from summer cuttings. Pruning is somewhat complex as is always the case with a large genus, and care must be taken not to over-prune. Those spiraeas that flower on the previous year's wood should only be pruned after flowering. Those that flower on new wood (generally the late flowerers) can be pruned in the early spring. In the first case, only a proportion of the wood should be removed in order to promote new growth. In the latter case, all the shoots, if necessary, can be cut to the ground.

Spiraea 'ARGUTA' (sometimes called 'BRIDAL WREATH') is a wonderful spring-flowering plant consisting of many arching, twiggy branches covered with masses of delicate, white flowers.

S. japonica (sometimes called S. × bumalda) is a small shrub between 1.2 and 1.5m (4 and 5ft) high. In the late summer it produces rose-pink flowers in flat-headed panicles. It has many varieties, among which are the following: 'ALBIFLORA' has white flowers; 'ANTHONY WATERER' has red flowers, but it is the new foliage that is of interest as it has a pink and cream variegation; 'GOLDFLAME' again has interesting foliage, this time leaves of reddish orange or yellow, paling to very light green; 'LITTLE PRINCESS' is a dwarf form with light green leaves, and 'SHIROBANA' has an interesting mixture of white and dark pink flowers.

S. nipponica is an early, white-flowering species. It has two forms of note: 'SNOW-MOUND', which has masses of larger flowers, and S.n. tosaensis, which is compact but less inclined to flower.

S. thunbergii has thin arching stems covered in white flowers in the spring. This makes a good hedge and is an excellent plant.

S. × vanhouttei is similar, except that the white flowers are held in clusters.

Styrax

JAPANESE SNOWBELL

THESE ARE EXTREMELY BEAUTIFUL, medium-sized trees whose charm lies in the white flowers that appear in early summer. They look like five-petalled snowdrops hanging from along the length of the branches. Later the petals open wide, revealing yellow anthers. The leaves are a light green, just the right colour to set off the freshness of the flowers. The tree slowly grows to about 7m (24ft), though some have a more shrubby nature. As it is only reasonably hardy, taking temperatures down to −10°C (14°F) or so, it would be advisable to give it some protection in colder areas. This is quite a large genus of 130 or so species, but there are only a handful in cultivation, Styrax japonica undoubtedly being the best.

These plants prefer a fairly light soil, preferably on the acidic side. They prefer full sun, but a little shade will be tolerated.

Styrax

Zone 8

They are beautiful trees and should be treated as specimen plants, to be sited by themselves or against a green background.

Propagation takes place from seed. No pruning is required.

Styrax americana is a shrubby form, reaching about 2m (6ft).

S. hemsleyana forms a tree with slightly larger flowers. These are not pendulous and are not as graceful as the next plant.

S. japonica is the pick of the bunch and is the species described at the beginning of this section. It is hardier and more commonly available than the other forms.

S. obassia is a taller tree than most, with rounder leaves. Its flowers are fragrant.

Syringa vulgaris

Styrax japonica

Syringa

S   A   W

Zone 8

Syringa

LILAC

LILAC IS ANOTHER OF those plants remembered from childhood that I could not conceivably be without. The smell of those elegant purple spires transports me to another world: spring would simply not be spring without it. Most people know the common lilac, *Syringa vulgaris*, that appears in a range of mauves and purples, but many are probably unaware of the other species, several of which have a lot to offer. They are all deciduous, with mainly ovate leaves. The flowers are small, tubular and four petalled, held in large spikes. The dominating colour is lavender blue or lilac, but other, darker colours have been introduced. The majority are fragrant. They form medium-to-large shrubs, sometimes growing to small trees. They are generally very hardy and should be no problem in most areas.

Lilacs are happy on most soils, including chalk. Full sun is appreciated, but they will tolerate some shade.

They grow easily and can go anywhere, either as specimen plants or mixed in with other shrubs and herbaceous plants. Out of its flowering season, lilac has not got much going for it, so it is best situated towards the back of a

Syringa microphylla

border. If you adore the fragrance, as I do, then it will have to be nearer to a path, both for smelling and cutting.

Propagation is from late-spring cuttings or from grafting. No pruning is required, though suckers must be removed, but should the plant get too leggy it can be cut back, as lilacs regenerate well from old wood.

Syringa × chinensis, the Rouen Lilac, is a dense bush with panicles of soft lilac flowers that are very fragrant. It has several cultivars of which 'SAUGEANA' is possibly the best and certainly the widest available. This last has much darker, reddish flowers.

S. × hyacinthiflora is a series of early hybrids produced in France. They are very floriferous and have larger panicles of flowers than usual. The young leaves are bronzy. Their main advantage is that they flower slightly earlier than other forms. There are several varieties still available, including doubles.

S. × josiflexa 'BELLICENT' is one of a series of Canadian hybrids that has very large, loose plumes of rose-pink flowers. Another is 'GUINEVERE', which has darker, purple flowers.

S. meyeri 'PALIBIN' forms a dense, small shrub. The flower panicles are quite short and a pinky lilac. It is very slow growing.

S. microphylla is a small shrub, less than 3m (6ft) high, with small leaves. It has small

Syringa × persica

Syringa × josiflexa 'BELLICENT'

panicles of pale lavender flowers in the spring, but often gives a smaller, second flush in autumn. 'SUPERBA' is the form usually grown.

S. × persica is another small bush, this time with narrow leaves. The loose panicles are not very large and contain small, mauve flowers. There is a white form, 'ALBA'.

S. reflexa is a medium-sized shrub with hairs on the undersides of the dark green leaves. The flowers are purple pink, held in drooping panicles.

S. vulgaris, Common Lilac, can rise up to 6m (20ft). It is the wild form and its flowers are a lilac colour. A large number of forms have been bred, however, with a colour range extending to deep purple. Many of these forms are doubles. 'CHARLES JOLY' is a purple-red double. 'KATHERINE HAVEMEYER' has large panicles of double lavender flowers. 'MADAME LEMOINE' is a very good double white. 'MICHEL BUCHNER' is another double, this time with purplish flowers. 'MRS EDWARD HARDING' is a purple-red double. 'PRIMROSE' is, unusually, a pale yellow, single form. 'SOUVENIR DE LOUIS SPAETH' is a single with wine-red trusses of flowers. 'VESTALE' is a single white.

Tamarix ramosissima

Tamarix

		✓
	✓	
✓		

Sp (S) (A) *W*

Zone 8

Tamarix

TAMARISK

A GROUP OF SHRUBS that are valuable for their ability to grow by the sea, tamarisks are characterized by their arching branches covered in tiny pink flowers, creating a very feathery appearance. The foliage consists of very small, scale-like leaves. They form medium-height shrubs of up to 4m (13ft), although some can get much larger. They are reasonably hardy, taking temperatures down to −10°C (14°F) or so, but this should be no problem in most seaside localities.

Tamarisks are tolerant towards most soils, including saline ones. They must be exposed to the full sun.

This is a background plant, either in a shrubbery or on a boundary. Several planted together produce a good effect, particularly if intermingled with purple-leaved plants.

Propagation from cuttings is extremely easy, and these can be taken at any time of year. No pruning is necessary unless you want neat tidy bushes, in which case the later-flowering varieties need pruning in early spring and the early varieties immediately after flowering.

Tamarix parviflora, as the name suggests, has small flowers that are rose pink in colour. It flowers in late spring.

T. ramosissima (sometimes called *T. pentandra*) has pale rose-pink flowers that appear in late summer, on into autumn. 'PINK CASCADE' has darker pink flowers.

T. tetrandra is similar to the previous plant except that it flowers in the spring.

Viburnum

VIBURNUM

THIS IS A LARGE genus, containing many very useful shrubs. They are particularly valuable in the early part of the year, several actually flowering throughout the winter. It is the flowers that make this group interesting: in spite of the variation of leaf shapes and the fact that some are deciduous and others evergreen, these are rather dull plants out of flower. But when they are in flower, all else is forgiven. The flowers are mainly white, often pink in bud, and are usually held in rounded or flat clusters. Quite a number are sweetly scented. Some species produce attractive fruit. They vary in stature between small and medium size, which makes them very suitable for a small garden. The majority are totally hardy.

There do not seem to be any problems with soils, many viburnums growing well on chalk. One of their useful qualities is that they prefer

Viburnum tomentosum 'PLICATUM'

a bit of light shade although they will happily take full sun.

Although there are some with interesting autumn colouring, viburnums are mainly grown for their flowers and their scent. The winter-flowering ones are particularly valuable and should be placed where you can appreciate them without wading through mud. Some of the evergreen varieties, particularly *V. tinus*, which flowers throughout the winter and into spring, make very good screens and informal hedges. Their ability to thrive in light shade is useful if you have north-facing borders to contend with. In spite of the dullness of a lot of viburnums when they are not in flower, they still make very good plants for the mixed border, particularly those with a more arching habit. The white and pinks of the flowers allow them to mix in virtually anywhere.

Propagation is generally from summer cuttings, although several species can be easily layered. Most need no pruning beyond being kept tidy, but some need to have a certain amount of the old wood removed from time to time in order to promote new growth.

Viburnum 'ANNE RUSSELL' is a very sweet-smelling, spring-flowering form. The flowers are pink in bud and white in flower. It is a compact evergreen shrub with glossy leaves.

V. betulifolium is a rather large shrub,

Viburnum tinus

Viburnum × *bodnantense*

Viburnum

Sp S A W
Zone 7

producing white flowers in early summer but mainly grown for its attractive bright red berries.

V. × *bodnantense* is a wonderful plant in that it has clusters of pink flowers from late autumn right through the winter. They are very fragrant. The shrub itself is a bit stiff and awkward looking, but the flowers are marvellous during those winter months. There are several forms available.

V. × *burkwoodii* is a very good free-flowering hybrid. It carries sweet-smelling white flowers from late winter into the spring. It is semi-deciduous. The form, 'PARK FARM', has pinker flower buds and some autumn colour.

V. × *carlcephalum* has tight round balls of fragrant flowers in spring. They are pink in bud, changing to white as they open.

V. carlesii is a rounded, deciduous shrub with very fragrant flowers in spring. The flowers are white, coming from pink buds. This is a marvellous shrub but it has tended to be overshadowed by some of the hybrids that have been developed from it, such as *V.* × *burkwoodii*. Several cultivars are available.

V. cinnamomifolium is a large, evergreen shrub with deeply veined leaves. The loose panicles of white flowers appear in early summer. It is similar to the following species, but not as good.

V. davidii is a compact evergreen shrub with

Viburnum × opulus

leathery, deeply veined leaves. It is one of the few viburnums that is grown for its leaves rather than its flowers. The latter are white and form in dense clusters in early summer.

V. farreri (still occasionally called *V. fragrans*) is another winter-flowering form with very sweet-smelling pinkish white flowers. This remains a wonderful winter plant but it has been superseded by *V. × bodnantense*.

V. × juddii is another of the *V. carlesii* hybrids, with loose, rounded clusters of white flowers in spring. The flowers are scented.

V. lantana has flat clusters of white flowers in late spring. The deciduous leaves colour in autumn and there are clusters of red berries.

V. opulus is the European Guelder Rose. This has delicate, lacecap flowers. These are flat white heads with small fertile flowers in the middle, surrounded by large infertile ones. These are followed in autumn by bunches of translucent red berries. There are several forms available, including some, such as 'STERILE', with round snowballs of flowers. Others, such as 'XANTHOCARPUM', have orange berries. 'AUREUM' has yellow foliage.

V. plicatum, Japanese Snowball, has either round balls or large flat plates of white flowers.

The leaves are ovate, with a pleasing pleated surface. This can be a splendid bush, particularly in some of its forms, such as 'MARIESII', which has tier upon tier of flat flower heads. There are several other forms: 'LANARTH' also has flat plates of flowers but the branches are less horizontal, thus losing some of the grace of 'MARIESII', while 'NANUM' is a more compact shrub. In 'PINK BEAUTY' the outer florets change to pink as they age. 'ROWALLANE' is a more compact bush, with large flowers, and is a good fruiting form.

V. rhytidophyllum has rather dirty white flowers in rounded clusters in spring, these having been carried as buds from the previous autumn. The evergreen leaves have a rough surface and hang dejectedly in frosty weather. This plant is best in full sun.

V. sargentii has white, lacecap flowers with purple anthers. It is a good fruiting species, producing clusters of translucent red berries.

V. tinus, Laurustinus, is a very versatile evergreen. It carries flowers in pink bud throughout the winter, when just a few open, but all finally open completely in spring. The flowers are held against dark green foliage. *V. tinus* makes a marvellous screen or even a hedge. Unfortunately it is not scented. There are several forms available.

V. tomentosum is a deciduous shrub with large heads of white flowers.

Viburnum × burkwoodii

Vinca

PERIWINKLE

PERIWINKLES DO NOT FORM shrubs or bushes in the conventional sense, but are nonetheless shrubby. This group of carpeting plants is very useful for ground cover, their charm lying in the bright blue, star-shaped flowers that shine upwards from the mass of ever-green leaves. Flowering starts in spring and continues for most of the summer, and they are completely hardy.

Periwinkles seem happy on most types of soil. They will tolerate either sun or quite dense shade, although in the latter position they are rather shy of flowering.

They can be used as ground cover in shady as well as sunny positions, but the latter is needed if they are to perform well. Sunny banks make an ideal situation. In my own garden, I have *V. major* growing through a hedge; the foliage is almost obscured but the flowers peek out in an almost cheeky way – a very lovely effect.

Periwinkles are easily propagated by layering; indeed, the plant frequently layers itself, to such an extent that this can become a nuisance, so there are usually plenty of spare plants. No pruning is necessary – it is more a matter of keeping the plant within bounds.

Vinca difformis is not a very common plant

Vinca minor

Vinca

Zone 7

but is well worth finding because it flowers non-stop from late autumn through to the next spring, often into the summer. The flowers are very pale blue, almost white. This species does not run as much as the others. It is reputed to be more tender than the others but it has stood winters of − 14°C (7°F) or more in my garden without any trouble.

V. major is similar but larger in all its parts than the following species. It makes excellent ground cover but also has a tendency to scramble through other bushes. It should be kept away from borders because the arching stems root very easily, enabling it to travel fast. There are several forms, 'VARIEGATA' being the commonest. This has creamy variegations to the leaf margins.

V. minor is a smaller version of the previous plant. It has some excellent cultivars. Among these is 'ALZA', which has white flowers. 'ALBA VARIEGATA' has white flowers and the additional benefit of creamy, variegated leaves. 'ARGEN-TEO-VARIEGATA' has yellow variegated leaves. 'ATROPURPUREA' has rich purple flowers, instead of the more usual blue. 'BOWLES VARIETY' has clear, light blue flowers, while 'GERTRUDE JEKYLL' has small white flowers.

Vinca major

Weigela florida 'VARIEGATA'

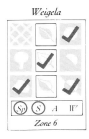

Weigela

Zone 6

Weigela

WEIGELA

THIS IS A SMALL GROUP OF SHRUBS that are widely available and are popular plants for the small garden. They are at their height in late spring and early summer, when they produce masses of flared funnels in a range of colours that are mainly pinks and reds, but also include white and yellow. The foliage is deciduous and consists of medium-sized ovate leaves. Weigelas grow up to about 2m (7ft). They are completely hardy.

They will grow on any soil. Full sun is appreciated but they will tolerate a little shade.

Weigelas are very useful shrubs in that they will fit virtually anywhere. A lot of the foliage is nondescript, but some, *W. florida* 'VARIEGA-TA' in particular, have foliage that is attractive and maintains its interest throughout the summer and autumn. These are perfectly at home in the mixed border.

Propagation from summer cuttings is easy. Pruning should be restricted to cutting back the flowering stems as soon as they have fulfilled their function, but if it is necessary to cut a plant back drastically it will come back the following season.

Weigela 'ABEL CARRIERE' has rose-carmine flowers with golden speckling in the throat.

W. 'BRISTOL RUBY' has good ruby-red

Weigela 'BRISTOL RUBY'

PURPUREIS' has deep pink flowers and purple-flushed leaves and is a smaller plant than some of the others.

W. 'LOOYMANSII AUREA' has pale pink flowers, with golden yellow leaves in spring, turning lime green as they age.

W. middendorffiana has more bell-shaped flowers that are pale yellow with orange markings.

W. 'NEWPORT RED' has bright red flowers.

W. 'PRAECOX VARIEGATA' has rose-pink flowers with yellow markings. It is sweetly scented and has cream-edged leaves.

flowers. It is one of the best forms.

W. 'CANDIDA' has pure white flowers.

W. 'EVE RATHKE' is one of the parents of 'BRISTOL RUBY'. It, too, has rich red flowers, but is not such a big plant.

W. florida is the main species in cultivation. The species itself is not so widely grown as many of its popular forms. The best form, indeed the best weigela many would say, is 'VARIEGATA'. It has quite small pink flowers and very good green and yellow foliage. Other forms of interest include 'BRISTOL SNOW-FLAKE', which has blush-pink flowers. 'FOLIIS

Wisteria

WISTERIA

THESE ARE INDEED HANDSOME plants. A sizeable wisteria in full bloom, with hundreds of large blue racemes hanging beneath the airy pinnate leaves, sends the pulse racing. Unfortunately you cannot rush out and buy a fully grown tree to wrap round your house; it takes time and patience. The flowers are typical of the pea family, Leguminosae, to which wisteria belongs. They erupt in spring in long chains; these are similar to laburnum, except that here the flowers are a soft blue. The different forms include whites as well as

Wisteria

Zone 6

Weigela middendorffiana

Wisteria sinensis

several minor variations on the lilac-blue theme. The foliage is like ash leaves, with several small leaflets along a central stem (this is called a pinnate leaf). The trunks become old and gnarled as they age and add to the character of the plant. All wisterias are fairly hardy, though you should seek advice when choosing a species for a cool zone. And a sunny wall is beneficial: this is for better flowering, rather than for protection from winter cold.

They are not too fussy about the kind of soil in which they grow as long as it is reasonably well drained. Do not over-feed.

The classic place for wisteria is along the walls of a house, but it can be supported on any form of structure, including trellises, archways, pergolas or even trees. They can in fact also be trained as standard trees. Occasionally, nurseries have plants which have been trained in this manner, but these are expensive.

Propagation is by layering in spring or taking late-summer cuttings. Grafting can also be used for some of the special forms.

Wisteria floribunda is one of the two main species. Its flowers are darker then those of *W. sinensis* and are up to 25cm (10in) in length. This species can easily be distinguished from its rival by the clockwise twist to its stems; *W. sinensis* goes the other way. There are quite a number of forms available. 'ALBA' has white

Wisteria floribunda 'MULTIJUGA'

Wisteria floribunda 'ALBA'

Yucca

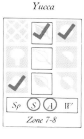

Yucca

Zone 7-8

YUCCA

I ALWAYS FEEL THESE look decidedly alien in most temperate landscapes but, at a second glance, they never fail to impress me. They are certainly distinct from any other shrub in this book, with their tropical elegance. The large flowering stem is covered with immense, creamy white bells hanging from lateral branches towering above an erect forest of stiff, pointed leaves. The top flowers can be 3m (10ft) or more above the ground. This is a very spectacular plant, especially when the sun is shining on it. In spite of coming from a warm climate yucca can stand quite a degree

Yucca whipplei

flowers. 'ISSAI' has free-flowering, lilac blossoms that are not very large, but this plant has the temporary advantage of flowering while still quite young. 'ISSAI PERFECT' has much longer racemes and is just as free-flowering. 'MULTIJUGA' has some of the longest racemes, reaching in excess of a metre (3ft). 'ROSEA' has pink and purple flowers.

W. sinensis is the other main species available. The racemes of this species are generally longer than those of *W. floribunda* (excepting 'MULTIJUGA'), up to 30cm (1ft) or more. The flowers also have the advantage over their relation in that all the flowers in the raceme open at the same time. They are generally lilac in colour, although there are quite a number of colour forms. 'ALBA' has white, very fragrant flowers. 'BLACK DRAGON' has double purple flowers. What a sensation they would be if they really were black! 'PLENA' has double flowers in the usual lilac colour. 'PROLIFIC' is a very free-flowering form. You may have to wait up to ten years before your first flowers appear, but it will be well worth it.

of frost, down to −12°C (10°F).

These shrubs can be planted in any sort of soil, as long as it is free draining. They must have full sun.

Care must be taken when placing yuccas in the garden. It is possible to capitalize on their vertical emphasis and their difference from anything else in the garden. A yucca makes an eye-catching focal point and can offset the hummocky nature of the rest of a border. Yuccas can also be used as specimen plants, standing by themselves, but I feel that this draws too much attention to them: they are quite capable of drawing their own attention, even when in the company of other plants, and need no further emphasis. They can be planted in tubs.

Propagation is from seed or rooted divisions. No pruning is required.

Yucca filamentosa is the most popular species available. In high summer, it bears creamy-white, bell-shaped flowers, between 5 and 7.5cm (2 and 3in) long, held on erect, plume-like panicles. These flower spikes may be as much as 2m (6ft) high, raised well above the 1-1.2m (3 to 4ft) mound of the plant itself – a dramatic and lovely sight. The "filamentosa" is a reference to the white threads that curl down from the edges of the stiffly erect leaves, which are glaucous and mid-green in colour. It has a form 'VARIEGATA', that has cream variations to the leaves.

Yucca gloriosa 'NOBILIS'

Y. flaccida is another popular species with several forms. This also has threads on the margins of the leaves, but in this case the tips of the leaves curl as well as the threads. Two main varieties are available: 'GOLDEN SWORD' has a yellowish stripe on the leaves, but 'IVORY' is better known. The mian attribute of the latter is that it is very free flowering.

Y. gloriosa has a long stem, this time the creamy white bells are tinged with deep pink on the outside. There is also a variegated form.

Y. recurvifolia, as its name suggests, has recurved leaves. It is about a metre (3ft) tall.

Y. whipplei is one of the taller yuccas, growing up to 4m (13ft). It has fragrant, greenish white flowers edged with purple.

Yucca gloriosa 'VARIEGATA'

Zenobia

ZENOBIA

IT IS NICE to be able to finish the list of plants with this delightful plant, which, for some reason, is not that well known. The genus is monotypic, the only species being *Zenobia pulverulenta*. It forms a small bush of little more than a metre (3ft) high. It has an open

Zenobia pulverulenta

character, with pure white flowers that hang from the ends of the branches. These flowers are similar to lily-of-the-valley in shape but smell of aniseed. They appear in summer. The bush is semi-evergreen, with more or less ovate leaves that have a bluish bloom. Those leaves that do eventually drop in autumn first turn a good red colour. Zenobia is only hardy down to about −10°C (14°F), so it will need some protection in the colder regions. It is also susceptible to wet conditions.

There has to be some drawback with such a desirable shrub and there is − it must have lime-free soil. The earth should also be moisture retentive, for zenobia does not like conditions too dry. It much prefers light shade: fortunately, as this is a low shrub, shade is not difficult to provide.

The shrub border is the ideal position for this plant, particularly if mixed with other lime haters, such as rhododendrons.

Zenobias can be propagated from summer cuttings or from layering. No pruning is required except for the removal of the flowering stems.

Zenobia

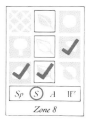

Sp ⓢ *A* *W*

Zone 8

GETTING THE BEST FROM YOUR TREES AND SHRUBS

SITING TREES AND SHRUBS

THERE CAN BE FEW PLANTS that have the versatility of trees and shrubs. They provide a garden with a sense of shape, texture and colour throughout the year. They can be used purely for their decorative effect, or as boundary hedging or screening for unsightly objects and areas. There are low growing shrubs that clothe the ground, forming an effective ground cover, and tall trees that catch the eye as a focal point to the garden. They will act as windbreaks, or provide shade for shade-loving plants. Not only decorative in their own right, they will also form a background against which other plants may be displayed at their best.

Trees and shrubs often become permanent residents in a garden: unlike many herbaceous plants they tend to live for a long time. In a lot of cases, particularly with trees, it may be many years before the plant has sufficiently established itself to come into flower. Both these factors, plus the great difficulty of moving such large and spreading plants once they have become established, means that great care must be exercised over siting and planting.

When a *Davidia involucrata* flowers for the first time after, say, twenty years, it is a bit late to decide that the colour is wrong for that position: to start again would mean that one would have to wait another twenty years.

Another general point to bear in mind is that trees and shrubs can grow into very large plants, not only in height and girth but in their underground parts, which can develop into an extensive network of hungry and thirsty roots. So much more care is needed when selecting and planting trees than in the case of any other type of plant. You must give the matter careful consideration.

General layout

It is rather presumptuous for an author to tell readers how to lay out their gardens. Garden design is very much a personal matter, but it is not something that is done very frequently and there are people who like to have advice. All the same, the choice of plants and the general atmosphere of a garden is a matter of personal taste, in the same way that the design of the interior of a house reflects the taste of the occupants. You are the person who has to live with your garden and like it. The choice of colours; the balance between flowers and greenery, and between lawn and borders or other features; all should be in tune with your taste and lifestyle. In a sense, trees and shrubs can be likened to the exterior fabric of the house: once they are established, they are permanent, short of a major upheaval.

The number of different shapes of gardens is infinite and so, consequently, is the number of possible garden designs. The basic message for anyone designing a garden is to keep it simple. This is particularly important in the smaller garden, where over-planting or convoluted lines will create a fussy and overdressed look. Restrict straight lines to boundary hedges; simple curves are more attractive elsewhere.

Even in a comparatively small garden,

shrubs can be used to provide a sense of drama and adventure by obscuring sections of the garden, which suddenly come into view as a corner is turned.

Winter flowering shrubs and trees can be ugly during the summer, so they should not be planted in a prominent position. On the other hand, they should ideally be placed where they can be seen from the house or from a path; it is no good having to traipse through the winter mud to see them.

Trees can grow very big and their number should be carefully controlled in the smaller garden. Avoid planting them too near the house, and remember that they will eventually cast a large amount of shade.

Below is listed a number of ways that trees and shrubs are often used.

Shrubberies

Shrubberies are now considered old-fashioned and, except in large gardens, it is rare to see borders devoted purely to shrubs. But with careful selection, a shrubbery can provide a trouble-free yet attractive addition to any garden, offering colour for most of the year; something that is very difficult to achieve with a pure herbaceous border. When planting out the shrubs, remember the eventual size and shape of the mature plants and leave plenty of space between them. If necessary, use temporary infillings, of heathers or herbaceous plants, for example.

Mixed and herbaceous borders

More common than shrubberies, mixed borders, as their name suggests, are a mixture of different types of plants: shrubs, herbaceous and even annual and bedding plants. Strictly speaking, herbaceous borders are restricted to herbaceous plants, but some shrubs such as fuchsias, buddleias and elders are cut to the ground each year and in many ways are treated as herbaceous plants. They certainly suit the feel and appearance of such borders. Shrubs fit into both types of border, giving them a more permanent structure and framework, and often providing a little light shade for those plants that require it.

Hedges

Used either on the boundary to a garden or as a division within it, hedges can either be kept tightly clipped and formal, which generally precludes any flowering, or informal, with arching flowering stems. The latter type of hedge takes up quite a lot of room and should be restricted to the larger garden. It still needs a degree of attention, including pruning, so it cannot be planted as an excuse to avoid hedge maintenance.

When planting hedges, always remember that a fast-growing one will always be fast growing; it will not stop when it has reached the required height. The faster a hedge reaches maturity, the more frequently it will require trimming or pruning. Some of the flowering prickly shrubs, such as berberis, make very good informal but attractive hedges, but be careful where they are used; for example as a screen to a swimming pool a berberis hedge could be disastrous, as the sharp spines seem to get everywhere.

Screens

Screens have many uses in a garden. Even the best of gardens will have some unsightly spots – garage, dustbins, compost heap – and judiciously placed shrubs can easily mask them. It is best to use evergreen shrubs, which maintain the disguise throughout the winter.

Walls and fences

Walls are often clothed with shrubs or climbers, for several reasons. A wall or fence may afford admirable protection to some of the more tender shrubs during the winter, and it can be a good foil to set off the flowers or foliage of the plant. Walls and fences add a vertical emphasis to a garden, they act as a solid support for climbing plants and, conversely, they are sometimes ugly – new fences, in particular, tend to look harsh and obtrusive until they have become weathered – and need plants to hide or soften them.

Good anchor points and wire or trellising should be fitted to the walls to give the plants firm support. If the walls have to be painted regularly, choose plants that can be eased away to allow access or that can be cut to the ground periodically.

Pergolas and trellises

These are essentially like walls, but less substantial. They are much lighter and more delicate in appearance and can be placed anywhere in a garden, acting as screens, dividers or archways from one area to another. When clothed with plants, they can have considerable wind resistance, so they should be strongly built to avoid being blown over.

Specimen plants

These are trees or shrubs that look better if placed by themselves rather than massed with others. They may form the focal point at the end of a vista or path, or they can stand alone on an expanse of lawn. Place such plants with great care, as the purpose of their isolation is to make them stand out and it can be disastrous if, when they are mature, it is decided that they have been wrongly sited.

SOIL AND CLIMATE

TWO VERY IMPORTANT FACTORS must be taken into account when considering the choice and siting of trees and shrubs: the soil and the weather.

Soil conditions

Soil can vary in both its chemistry and its structure. Most trees and shrubs will grow on neutral or acid soils, as long as the latter is not too acidic. Alkaline or chalky soils present more of a problem. Some plants, such as rhododendrons or pierises, will not tolerate any alkalinity: a few will turn up their toes if they are irrigated with hard water, even though they are planted in acidic soils. Many others will tolerate a certain amount of alkalinity but will become chloritic (with leaves turning yellow) and stunted if the levels are too high.

If you live on limy or chalky soil, you will either have to forgo the lime-hating plants (there are still plenty of others from which to choose) or grow the smaller species in contain-ers or special beds, containing imported neutral or acidic soil. The beds should preferably be constructed above the surrounding soil level or lime will eventually leach into them, killing off or maiming the plants.

Soil-testing kits can be bought very cheaply and will allow you to discover which type of soil you have. These kits indicate the pH level of the soil: $pH7$ is neutral; the higher you go above this figure the more alkaline the soil, and the lower you go the more acid.

The extremes of physical structure are sandy soils and clay soils. The former presents problems to the gardener because its light structure dries out very quickly and contains little of nutritional value. A sandy soil requires feeding heavily with compost, manure and peat to give it bulk and the ability to retain moisture. Clay soils are the opposite; they are heavy and sticky. They are very moisture-retentive in wet seasons, but if they dry out they become rock hard. This is a very difficult soil to work. Again, plenty of organic material is a great help, as is the addition of horticultural grit or sharp sand, which helps to break down the clay structure. With time and patience, a clay soil can be converted to a loamy one, which is the ideal. Loam is a balanced mixture of clay and sand, and is porous yet moisture-retentive.

Weather conditions

There are three aspects of the weather to take into account: sun, wind and frost.

Look carefully at the entries in this book before siting a tree or shrub, because some will only grow in full sun, while others prefer shady conditions. There is no problem with the former, but the latter can vary considerably. Very few plants will tolerate full shade; dappled shade is preferable. This can be achieved by planting near or under another tree or shrub that is larger but that does not cast too dense a shade. More preferable still are north-facing positions (south-facing in the southern hemisphere), where the sun is excluded but there is ample light from above. Many plants will tolerate either sun or shade, but as a general rule they will not flower as well in shade. They might also get drawn; their shape being weedy and out of character.

Windy sites should be given some form of protection. In the early stages of a garden this might well take the form of plastic netting designed for the purpose, but shelter belts of wind-resistant trees and shrubs should be planted as soon as possible. Ornamental trees and shrubs can be severely damaged by strong winds, particularly cold or salt-laden ones.

Hardiness to frost is another crucial thing to be borne in mind. Each plant in the book has been given a minimum temperature that it will tolerate and a hardiness zone number in which it will grow. Little can be done about frosts, except to site suspect plants in warmer parts of the garden, particularly against south walls (north in the southern hemisphere). Tender shrubs can also be cocooned in hessian, straw or bracken if frost is expected. Frost pockets can develop in some parts of a garden, particularly where the frost rolls down a hill and gets trapped by hedges or buildings. In the case of hedges, a well-placed gap will allow the frost to move on down the hill.

In some areas drought is another weather condition which may cause problems. In dry areas, organic material should be added to the soil to help retain moisture and the surface should be heavily mulched. Plants should also be watered regularly, particularly before they have become fully established.

CULTIVATION
Preparing the ground

BEFORE ANY TREE OR SHRUB IS PLANTED the site should be thoroughly prepared. It might be argued that, as nature does not prepare a site, we should just dig a hole and put the plant in. Unfortunately, however, out of every million seeds that nature sows, probably only one will reach maturity. The gardener, on the other hand, wants every one of his progeny to succeed, so they must be given the best chances. Site preparation is one of the ways of helping to ensure that they get these.

All perennial weeds should be thoroughly cleared away; there is nothing worse than trying to remove a persistent weed from among established shrubs, particularly if the latter are multiple stemmed or suckering. Beds should be well dug, preferably double dug, with plenty of organic material added. For isolated trees or shrubs a hole should be prepared. This should be at least a metre (3ft) wide – preferably more – and it should be dug to a minimum depth of 50cm (18in). Again, the soil should be weed free and organic material should be added.

Very few trees and shrubs like, or will tolerate, waterlogged conditions, so serious consideration should be given to drainage. Apart from bog plants there are few in the normal garden that like excess water, so drainage should be part of the overall plan. This can be achieved by soil improvement – in other words, the addition of grit and humus to break down the soil – or by the installation of a proper drainage system. If there is any risk that a hole prepared for a tree may turn into a water sump, then drainage channels should be cut, leading away from the hole.

Planting

Trees and shrubs that have been purchased bare rooted (dug straight from the ground) may be planted between autumn and the spring, providing the ground is not frozen. Container-grown plants can be planted at any time, again providing the ground is not frozen or baked hard. Periods when there are drying winds should also be avoided.

The ground should be thoroughly prepared, after which you should dig a hole wider than the extent of the roots. The depth of the hole should be adjusted so that the plant can rest at the same depth as in the pot or the nurseryman's plot. The roots of bare-rooted plants should be gently spread out and then good quality topsoil should be worked in between them. Make sure that you leave no air pockets or holes under or around the roots. Container plants should be watered an hour or so before planting. Roots should be gently teased out if the plant is pot-bound. In both cases the hole should be partially filled until the roots are just covered. After this the soil is gently firmed and the plant is well watered, so that the remaining hole is filled with water. The rest of the soil can then be replaced: mound it slightly round the stem of the plant; then allow a few hours for the excess water to drain away, then gently firm the soil down, adding extra soil if necessary to make the planted area level.

Trees, and shrubs in windy areas, should be staked. A stout post should be inserted into the hole before planting. It is better to do this before rather than after planting, to avoid damaging the roots. Adjustable rubber straps should be used to attach the plant to the stake. The tree should not touch the stake as it is likely to rub and cause damage. A more secure method is to use two stakes, each with a strap running around the tree trunk.

Aftercare

The ground around the tree or shrub should be kept free of weeds until the plant is established. Mulching with organic material or laying black plastic over the ground will not only help to keep the weeds down, but will also help to preserve water. Water is very crucial to a newly planted tree and the ground should not be allowed to go short of moisture. Bonemeal or a general fertilizer can be applied in early spring to feed the plant. The rubber straps on the supports should be adjusted periodically to prevent them eating into the tree. Once the tree has become established, the supports can be removed. Other than pruning (see below) little other attention is needed.

Pruning

This can be a worrying topic for many gardeners. They are never certain when to prune and how much to remove: consequently, trees and shrubs are often neglected and too little is cut off. On the other hand, some gardeners are butchers and hack away at everything. When in doubt, it is probably safer to err on the side of underpruning than to massacre your plants.

There are several reasons for pruning. The removal of dead wood is obviously important. Pruning can dictate the shape of the plant (an obvious example of this is a hedge). It

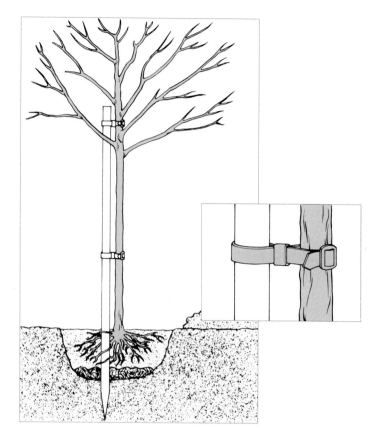

To avoid damaging the roots, the post should be inserted when you plant the tree. In windy areas, two stakes should be used so that the tree can be supported between them. Specially purchased rubber ties should be used to attach the tree to the supports. These should be adjusted as the tree grows and must be secure enough to prevent movement of the trunk.

can also affect the quantity of flowers produced by a tree or shrub and may even influence the flowering time. It will also help to promote new growth and can encourage the rejuvenation of the plant.

Pruning details for individual trees and shrubs are given under the entry for each in the main part of this book, but there are some basic principles that should be followed.

All trees and shrubs should have any dead or damaged wood removed. It is important to

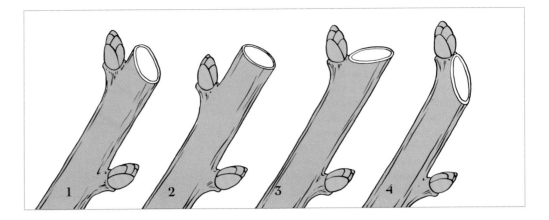

When pruning, cut just above a viable bud (**1**).
Cutting too far above the bud (**2**) *or too close to it*
(**4**) *will cause die-back. The cut should be carefully
angled at about 30 degrees, with the cut slanted
away from the bud* (**1**) *and not towards it* (**3**).

check them in spring, particularly if there have
been gales in the winter. Before starting to
prune or shape the plants at any other time of
year, it is again essential to take away any dead
material; once this has been removed you will
have a much better idea of what to do next. If
there are any branches that rub together, one
or the other should be removed (both if they
are damaged). Any weak growth should also
be taken out.

Pruning to promote flowering and rejuvenation usually takes the form of reducing
the number of flowering stems by about one
third, the oldest stems being chosen as the ones
for removal. This means that the shrub is
completely renewed every three years or so,
keeping it healthy and vigorous. Some shrubs,
as described below, need hard pruning. This
consists of cutting the plant right back to the
lowest growing points in the old wood.
Sometimes these may be only just above
ground level.

The pruning cut should be just above a
viable bud, at an angle of about 30 degrees to
the horizontal.

Fortunately there are many plants, especially trees, that need no pruning at all. If you

want a trouble-free life, these are the ones to
choose. Evergreen shrubs are less likely to
need pruning than deciduous ones. Some trees
and shrubs positively dislike being pruned
and, apart from the removal of dead wood,
these should be left alone.

As far as shrubs that require pruning are
concerned, there are two other broad catagor-
ies: those that flower on old wood and those
that flower on new wood. As a general
principle, the former should be pruned immediately after flowering, so that the new
growth has time to mature before the next
flowering season, and a third of the old wood
should be removed. Those shrubs that flower
on new growth should be pruned in the spring.
These should have the old flowering stems cut
back to the first growing bud. In some cases,
such as Buddleia, Fuchsia or Sambucus the
plants are cut right back almost to the ground
and treated as herbaceous plants. Reference to
the entries in the main part of this book will
give guidance as to the category to which
individual plants belong.

Some plants produce suckers. This may
be desirable if you want a shrubby thicket, but
if not then the suckers should be broken off at
the point at which they grow from the roots. If
they are cut off at ground level, this will
promote more suckers. Removal of suckers is
particularly important where the plant is not
growing from its own rootstock. The suckers
will resemble the stock and not the plant you
have selected.

PROPAGATION

MANY GARDENERS LIKE to propagate their own plants. Not only is this cheaper than buying trees and shrubs, but potentially it gives a wider choice of plants and also a great deal of satisfaction. As well as commercial firms, there are organizations who supply a vast range of seed, and gardeners are often generous with cuttings and other materials. Equally, it is a good thing, if you have a rare or a good form of a plant, to be able to propagate it and give it to others.

Seed

The simplest way of sowing seed for the garden is to scatter the seed thinly over a pot of seed compost and cover it with a 1cm (0.4in) layer of grit. Put the pot outside in a shady place and keep it moist.

Some tree and shrub seeds need a period of cold weather to break the dormancy. If you are in no hurry, let nature do this for you: simply leave the pot in the open until the seed germinates. On the other hand you can, if you wish, speed up the germination process by creating an artificial winter. To do this, put the pot in a domestic refrigerator for a couple of months before placing it outside.

The grit on the top of the pot helps to keep the seed in place, moist and weed free, and it also provides a dry collar round the neck of the seedling, which helps to prevent it rotting. Some seed may have to be kept in the pot for two or more years before it germinates.

The biggest problem with propagating from seed is that there is no guarantee that the resulting offspring will resemble the parent. Certainly, most cultivars will not breed true, and even many species may exhibit foreign influences due to itinerant bees. For faithful reproduction, one of the following methods must be used.

Cuttings

As well as bearing a true likeness to its parent, a plant grown from a cutting will establish itself quicker than one grown from seed. Not all trees and shrubs will easily reproduce them-selves in this way, but a great number will, as indicated under the individual entries in the main part of this book.

Cuttings are prepared simply by remov-ing a non-flowering shoot from the plant. The length of the shoot will vary according to subject, but choose material in which the joints are as close together as possible. I like to have a terminal bud of leaves, from one joint of which I remove the leaves. I cut under the final joint, having first removed its leaves. This final joint or node is then dipped in fresh rooting powder and placed in cutting compost (50 percent compost and 50 percent peat is ideal), either in a propagator or in a pot that can be covered with a polythene bag or some other transpa-rent cover. Depending on the length of the shoot, there may be more joints above or below ground.

Some plants root more easily if they have a "heel". This is a piece of old wood at the base of the cutting, taken from where the cutting joins the main stem.

Leaves are removed from the part of the stem that goes below the surface, to prevent rotting, and also above ground, to prevent the loss of too much water through transpiration. They should be removed cleanly with a sharp knife or razor blade. The topmost leaves are left on the plant, but if they are large they should be reduced by half by cutting cleanly with a razor.

The pots should be kept moist and out of direct sunlight, although they need as much light as possible. Rooting time varies, but the start of new growth from the nodes generally indicates that roots have been formed and it is time to pot your cuttings up into larger, individual containers. Some subjects, such as roses and other plants that root easily from large cuttings, can be inserted directly into the ground in a shady spot. The soil should be light and friable, and it must be kept moist.

Some plants respond from cuttings taken early in the year, when the growth is still soft (softwood cuttings). Other cuttings can be taken when the growth has firmed up and is quite hard (hardwood cuttings). These last are often taken in the autumn and are not potted

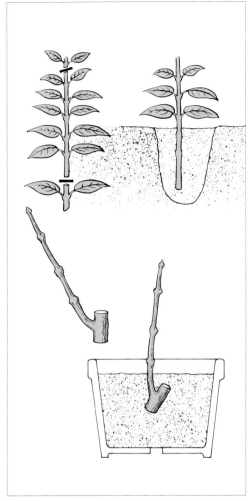

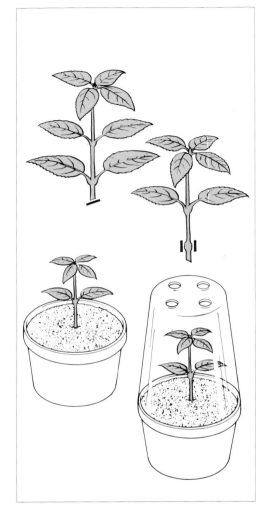

Softwood cuttings can be taken from the tips of growing shoots when the green growth is beginning to firm up. They should be trimmed with a razor or sharp knife just below a leaf node, forming a cutting of about 5-10cm (2-4in) depending on the plant. Remove the lower leaves, being careful to make a clean cut. If the leaves are very large they should be cut in half to reduce the transpiration rate and the consequent loss of water. The end of the cutting is dipped in rooting hormone and put in a mixture of sharp sand and peat. This is kept damp in a propagator or polythene bag until roots have formed.

Hardwood cuttings of about 25-30cm (10-12in) are taken in the autumn from the ripened wood of shoots produced during the year. The lower leaves are stripped off and any soft tips removed. The lower 7.5-10cm (3-4in) is placed in a pot or a shallow trench and bedded in with a sharp sand and peat mixture. A trench should be in a sheltered spot away from direct sunlight and should be kept moist. Thin shoots, such as those of berberis, can run out of food reserves before roots are formed: in this case take "mallet" cuttings, which include a portion of the old wood containing extra reserves, and insert them in pots.

up until the following year. Intermediate between these two are half-ripe – sometimes called semi-hardwood or first year mature – cuttings, usually taken in summer. The types of cuttings required to propagate different plants are given in the main part of this book.

Layering

This is a simple technique and can be a good way of propagating difficult plants, but it can take a long time. A stem is bent down from the parent plant and secured just beneath the surface of the soil, either with a peg or a heavy stone. A short cut is made at the centre of that part of the shoot that is below ground, and the tip is bent upwards and supported by a stake. Keep the layer moist. It is impossible to generalize on the time taken to root, some difficult subjects might take years, but new top growth will be a sign that the layer has rooted.

Grafting

For various reasons, it is often desirable to grow a tree or a shrub on the rootstock of another plant. It may be that the tree you want is too vigorous and that by growing it on a less vigorous rootstock it can be kept more compact or more dwarf. Sometimes, it is possible to grow two varieties on the same plant or to produce exciting chimeras such as + *Laburnocytisus*. There are several ways of grafting, and the technicalities deserve a book on their own. The keen gardener might like to undertake grafting himself, in which case he will have to pursue the subject in more detail than I can give here. Fortunately, there are several excellent books about grafting.

Division

This is a method normally associated with herbaceous plants, but a number of suckering bushes can be multiplied by removing a piece of the original plant, complete with roots, and planting it elsewhere.

Aftercare

Seedlings and cuttings should be potted up into a good potting compost as soon as they are strong enough to be handled. Avoid potting up

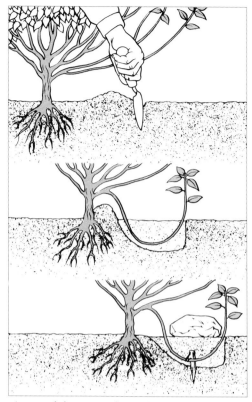

A stem of the parent plant is bent into a depression in the ground and covered with soil, or potting compost if the soil is poor. It is secured in position with a peg or heavy stone. The layer is kept moist and severed from the parent plant when roots have formed, which may take up to several years in some cases.

in winter, as cold weather can kill off the plant before it can resume growth. They should be potted on in increasing sizes of pots, preferably ones that are sufficiently deep to accommodate the long tap roots until the plants are large enough to plant out. Plants produced by layering or division can be planted straight out if they are big enough.

PESTS AND DISEASES

FORTUNATELY, TREES AND SHRUBS are not so prone to pests and diseases as many of the other garden plants. There are, however, a few common problems.

Pests

Aphids, or greenfly, suck the sap of new shoots, which can cause damage. They also produce a sticky honeydew that coats the leaves, making them unpleasant to touch. This honeydew is not harmful in itself, but it plays host to a minute black fungus, which gives the impression that the leaves are covered in a sooty deposit. This cuts down the amount of light reaching the leaves as well as looking unsightly. Aphids are generally not a sufficient nuisance (except possibly to some roses and honeysuckle) to warrant any special remedies. Where infestations are bad, one of the many proprietary insecticides can be used.

Birds, especially bullfinches, can peck out a lot of the emerging buds, often destroying the flowering potential of the plant, particularly spring-flowering species. The only real deterrent, apart from cats, is the tedious one of draping black cotton through the branches to deter the birds.

Caterpillars will happily chew petals or young leaves, making an unsightly mess, but unless the outbreak is severe it can be ignored.

Capsid bugs damage the young leaves, giving them a ragged, holed appearance. A systemic insecticide should reduce their activity if it becomes troublesome.

Deer will browse on shrubs and can cause substantial damage, particularly when other food-stuffs are in short supply. Unfortunately, there is little that can be done except to erect tall fences.

Earwigs can spoil the appearance of flowers by chewing the petals. This is not such a big problem with trees and shrubs as it is with other plants, but it can make a mess of some species, such as Clematis. Normally, this problem is not worth worrying about.

Rabbits can be a nuisance at the early stages of a tree's or shrub's life, when they will often eat the bark, killing the plant. Guards made from plastic or wire netting will protect the young trunk.

Diseases

Chlorosis, which is a disorder rather than a disease, is caused by the soil being too alkaline and preventing the absorption of minerals, particularly iron. The leaves turn yellow and look very sickly. There are chemical compounds that will give temporary relief, but unless the soil can be changed, the best solution is to relocate the plant, and set a more lime-tolerant tree or shrub in its place.

Coral spot is a small pinkish-red fungus which grows on dead branches. Branches bearing it should be cut out and burnt.

Honey fungus is one of the dreads of gardeners. Toadstools appear during the later half of the year around the base or above the roots of the affected plant. A brown rot soon sets in, particularly in the roots, and the plant dies. Black threads spread out from the dying plant and are likely to infect neighbouring plants. It is difficult to treat, but there are one or two proprietary fungicides which claim to help. All infected wood, including roots, should be burnt. No woody plants should be planted in the same ground for several years.

Leaf spot or **fungus leaf spot** is the commonest of the diseases. There are countless numbers of different fungi that cause this disfiguring complaint in which leaves develop yellow or brown patches or spots. Eventually, the whole leaf may be affected. Rose black spot is a familiar example. Spray with a fungicide if the attack is bad, and remove and burn all fallen leaves.

Powdery mildew is a common fungus, coating the leaves of the plant with a fine white powder. It is most common in damp areas with little air circulation, but conversely it is also caused by dryness around the roots. It debilitates the plant rather than killing it, and it can be successfully controlled by fungicides.

Rust is another fungal disease. This appears as small brown deposits on the leaves and can weaken the plant to a point where it dies. Spray affected plants with fungicide and burn all fallen leaves.

GLOSSARY

Acid soil Soil without any lime content, having a *pH* level of 6.5 or less.

Alkaline soil The opposite of *acid*: those soils that have a *pH* value of more than 7.4.

Anther The male part of a flower that carries the pollen.

Axil The angle between a leaf (or its stalk) and the stem. Buds formed in this angle are known as axillary buds.

Bare-rooted plants Plants that are dug up and sold direct from their nursery beds with their roots bared. Not sold in containers.

Bipinnate Leaves that are divided into leaflets, which in turn are also divided.

Bloom (*1*) Flower head (*2*) A fine powder-like covering on leaves and fruit.

Bracts Modified leaves which surround the flower. Bracts are often colourful, giving the impression that they are flower petals.

Bud A scaly swelling that contains a young shoot, leaf or flower.

Calyx Collective name for the ring of *sepals* that surrounds the petals of a flower before it opens.

Calcifuge A plant that does not like *alkaline* conditions.

Chlorosis A yellowing of leaves due to lack of minerals, usually caused by excess *alkalinity*.

Clone A group of identical plants that have been *vegetively propagated* from the same source.

Corolla The collective name for the petals.

Corymb A flat-headed flower head.

Cultivar A variety of a plant originating in cultivation as opposed to in the wild.

Cutting A piece of stem which is rooted to produce a new plant.

Damping off Death of seedlings due to the stems rotting at soil level.

Dioecius Having male and female flowers on separate plants. Both are required to achieve *pollination* and to assure fruit.

Division Method of *propagation* in which the plant is split into several parts.

Dormancy Period when seed is inactive, waiting for some stimulus to start it into growth.

Double flower Flowers that have more than the usual number of petals.

Evergreen A plant that has leaves all year round.

Fastigiate Having branches that grow almost vertically, parallel to the trunk.

Floret Individual flower in a compound flower head.

Friable soil Soil that is crumbly in texture.

Fungicide A chemical that kills fungal diseases.

Genus A grouping of plants having similar characteristics. It is subdivided into species and is represented by the first element in a botanical name.

Germination The first stage in the development and growth of a seed.

Glabrous Hairless.

Groundcover Plants used for covering large areas of soil. They are often planted to keep the weeds down.

Habit Overall shape of a tree or shrub. General appearance.

Hardwood cutting A *cutting* taken when the wood is fully ripe, usually in the latter part of the year.

Hardy Able to tolerate frost.

Herbicide A type of weedkiller.

Humus Decayed organic matter such as *leaf-mould*, garden compost or farmyard manure.

Hybrid A plant created by crossing two dissimilar parent plants.

Inflorescence Flower head or number of flowers on a stem.

Insecticide Chemical for killing insects.

Lanceolate Referring to leaves that are lance-shaped.

Lateral A shoot or branch coming out of the main stem or trunk.

Leader The top or leading shoot on a stem or branch.

Leaf-mould Partially decayed leaves, useful for incorporating in the soil as *humus*.

Linear Referring to leaves that are long and narrow.

Mulch A cover of organic material placed around the plant to help to retain moisture in the soil and restrict weed growth.

Neutral Soil that is neither acid nor alkaline.

Ovate Referring to oval-shaped leaves.

Palmate Referring to leaves with sections that radiate like fingers on a hand.

Panicle A branched flower head.

Pedicel A flower stalk to an individual flower.

Peduncle A flower stalk either to a cluster or a solitary flower.

Pesticide A chemical for killing insects

Petiole A leaf stalk.

pH A scale of *acidity/alkalinity*.

Pinnate A compound leaf which is divided into leaflets on either side of a central stalk.

Pollination The fertilization of a flower by the transfer of pollen from the male to female parts of the flower.

Procumbent Low growing; creeping.

Propagation Increasing the number of plants by artificial means.

Prostrate Low growing.

Raceme A flower head in the form of a spike.

Sap The juice of a tree or shrub.

Scion A part of a plant that is grafted onto a rootstock.

Sepals Leaf-like parts of the flower that act as protection for the petals and inner part of the flower. Collectively known as the *calyx*.

Sessile Having no stalks. Can refer either to flowers or leaves.

Species An individual unit or closely related group of plants within a *genus*.

Specimen plants Trees and shrubs with qualities that make them ideal for planting on their own.

Sport A chance shoot that is different in leaf or flower from the rest of the plant. The shoot can be *vegetatively propagated* and hence form a new cultivar.

Stamen The male part of the flower containing the *anther*.

Standard A single-stemmed shrub or tree.

Stigma The female part of a flower, on which the pollen is deposited.

Stolon Underground shoot which produces a new plant when it surfaces.

Sucker A shoot, other than the main stem, growing from an underground part of the plant.

Tender Plants unable to withstand frosts.

Trifoliate Leaves divided into three parts.

Type-plant A plant typical of that *species* in the wild.

Umbels A rounded or flat-topped flower head.

Variegated Leaves with areas of two or more colours.

Variety Any distinct form of *species* or *hybrid*.

Vegetative propagation *Propagation* by methods other than seed. Produces a plant identical to its parent.

INDEX

Page numbers in **bold** indicate illustrations

Abelia:
  'EDWARD GOUCHER' 10
  floribunda 10
  × *grandiflora* 10
  'COPPER GLOW' **10**
  schumannii 10
Abeliophyllum distichum 10-11, **11**
Abutilon:
  hybrids 12
  megapotamicum 11-12, **12**
  × *milleri* 12
  × *suntense* 12
  vitifolium 12
Acacia 12-13
  armata 12, 13
  baileyana 13, **13**
  dealbata 13
  longifolia 13
  melanoxylon 13
Acacia, False 120-1
Aesculus 13-15
  × *carnea* 14, **14**
  hippocastanum 14, **14**
  indica 14
  parviflora 15
  pavia 15
Almond 114
Alpine Bottle Brush 26
Alpine rose 118
Amelanchier:
  canadensis 15-16
  laevis 16
  lamarckii **15**, 16
Andromeda:
  glaucophylla 16
  polifolia 16, **16**
Angelica Tree 16-17
Aralia 16-17
  elata 17
  'AUREOVARIEGATA' **17**
Arbutus 17-18
  andrachne 18
  × *andrachnoides* 18
  menziesii 18
  unedo **17**, 18
Arctostaphylos:
  nevadensis 18
  uva-ursi 18, **18**
  'NANA' 18
Australian Bottle Brush 25-6
Azalea 116, 119

Banksia:
  coccinea 19, **19**
  ericifolia 19
  grandis 19
  serrata 19
  speciosa 19, **19**

Barberry 19-22
Bearberry 18
Beauty Bush 83-4
Bell Heather 52
Berberis 19-22
  aggregata 20
  buxifolia 20
  'NANA' 20
  darwinii 20, **20**, **21**
  gagnepainii 21
  julianae 21
  linearifolia 21
  ottawensis 21
  'SUPERBA' 21
  × *stenophylla* 21, **21**
  thunbergii 21
  'ATROPURPUREA' 21
  'ATROPURPUREA NANA' 21
  'AUREA' 21-2
  'GOLD RING' 21
  'ROSEGLOW' 21
  wilsoniae 22
Bird Cherry 114
Blackwood Acacia 13
Blue Mint Bush 29-30
Bluebush 54
Bog Myrtle 82
Bog Rosemary 16
Boronia:
  crenulata 22
  floribunda 22
  heterophylla 22, **22**
  megastima 22
  serrulata 22
Bottle Brush 25-6
Bougainvillea:
  × *buttiana* 23
  'APPLE BLOSSOM' 23, **23**
  'BRILLIANCE' 23
  spectabilis 23, **23**
Bramble 126-7
Broom 45-6, 64-5
  Spanish 130
Buckeye 13-15
Buddleia 23-5
  alternifolia 24, **24**
  colvilei 24
  crispa 24
  davidii 24
  fallowiana 24, **25**
  globosa **24**, 25
  × *weyeriana* 25
Butterfly Bush 23-5

Calico Bush 82
Californian Lilac 30-1
Californian Tree Poppy 121
Callistemon 25-6
  citrinus 26, **26**
  rigidus **25**, 26
  salignus 26

  sibieri 26
  viminalis 26
Calluna vulgaris 26-7
  v. alba 27
  v. 'AUREA' 27
  v. 'CUPREA' 27
  v. 'DARKNESS' **26**, 27
  v. 'GOLDEN FEATHER' 27
  v. 'H. E. BEALE' **27**, 27
  v. 'KINLOCHRUEL' 27
  v. 'ROBERT CHAPMAN' 27
  v. 'SILVER QUEEN' 27
  v. 'SUNSET' 27
Camellia 27-8
  japonica 28
  'ADOLPHE AUDUSSON' **27**
  'NOBILISSIMA' **28**
  × *williamsii*:
  'DONATION' **28**
  'J. C. WILLIAMS' **28**
Carpenteria californica 29, **29**
Caryopteris × *clandonensis* 29-30, **29**
Ceanothus 30-1
  arboreus 'TREWITHEN BLUE' **30**, 31
  'AUTUMNAL BLUE' 31
  × *delilianus* 'GLOIRE DE VERSAILLES' 31
  dentatus **30**, 31
  impressus 31
  thyrsiflorus 31, **31**
  'REPENS' 31
Ceratostigma willmottianum 31-2, **31**
Chaenomeles:
  japonica **32**, 33
  speciosa 33
  × *superba* 33
  'KNAP HILL SCARLET' **32**
  'NICOLINE' **32**
Cheal's Weeping Cherry 114
Cherry, Ornamental 113-15
Cherry Plum 114
Chimonanthus praecox 33, **33**
Chinese Witch Hazel 67
Choisya 33-4
  arizonica 34, **34**
  ternata 34, **34**
Christmas Box 127-8
Cinquefoil 110-11
Cistus 34-6
  × *aquilari* 35, **35**
  albidus **35**
  × *corbariense* 35
  × *cyprius* 35
  ladanifer **34**, 35-6
  laurifolius 36
  × *purpureus* 26
Clematis 36-8
  'BILL MACKENZIE' 38

  chrysocoma 38
  cirrhosa balearica 36, **36**
  'ELSA SPATH' (*C.* 'XERXES') 38
  jackmanii **37**, 38
  'SUPERBA' 38
  'MARIE BOISSELOT' ('MADAME LE COULTRE') 38
  montana 37, 38
  'ALBA' 38
  'ELIZABETH' 38
  'GRANDIFLORA' **37**
  'RUBENS' 38
  'NELLY MOSER' **36**, 38
  orientalis 38
  tangutica **38**, 38
  'VILLE DE LYON' 38
  viticella 38
  'ROYAL VELOURS' 38, 130
Clerodendrum 38-9
  bungei 39, **39**
  trichotomum 39
  fargesii 39
climate 147-8
Cobnut 43
Convolvulus:
  cneorum 39
  sabatius (*C. mauritanicus*) 39, **39**
Cootamundra Wattle 13
Coral Gum 55
Corkscrew Hazel 42
Cornel 40-1
Cornish Heath 53
Cornus:
  alba 40, 41
  canadensis 40-1, **40**
  florida 41
  'RUBRA' **40**
  kousa **40**, 41
  chinensis 41
  mas 41
  nuttalli 41, **41**
  stolonifera (*C. sericea*) 41
Corylopsis:
  pauciflora 41-2
  platypetala 42
  sinensis, var. *sinensis* (*C. willmottiae*) 42, **42**
  spicata 42
  veitchiana **41**, 42
  willmottiae 42, **42**
Corylus:
  avellana 42
  'CONTORTA' 42, **42**
  maxima 43
Cotinus:
  coggygria 43, **43**
  'FLAME' 43
  'FOLIIS PURPUREIS' 43
  'ROYAL PURPLE' **43**, 43
  obovatus (*C. americanus*) 43-4

Cotton Lavender 127
Crab Apple 98-100
Creeping Wintergreen 63
Crinodendron:
   hookeranum 44, **44**
   patagua 44
Cross-leaved Heath 53
Crowea 44-5
   angustifolia 45
   exalata 45
   saligna **44**, 45
Crown of Thorns 57
cultivation 148-50
cuttings 151-3, **152**
Cytisus 45-6
   battandieri **45**, 46
   × *beanii* 46
   × *kewensis* 46
   'LORD LAMBOURNE' **46**
   × *praecox* 46
   purpureus 46
   scoparius 45, **45**, **46**, 46

Daisy Bush 101-2
Daphne 46-8
   × *burkwoodii* 47, **47**
   cneorum 47
   mezereum 47-8, **47**
   odora 48
   tangutica 48
Davidia involucrata 48, **48**
Deutzia 48-9
   chunii 49
   × *elegantissima* 49
   gracilis 49
   × *hybrida* 49
   × *kalmiflora* 49, **49**
   × *magnifica* 49, **49**
   × *rosea* 49
   scabra 49
diseases 154
division 153
Dogwood 40-1
Dorset Heath 52
Dorycnium hirsutum 50, **50**
Dyer's Greenwood 64-5

Elisha's Tears 89
Embothrium coccineum 50-1, **50**
Erica 51-3
   arborea 52
     'CONTORTA' **52**
   australis 52
   ciliaris 52
   cinerea 52
     'ATRORUBENS' **51**
     'CEVENNES' **52**
   × *darleyensis* 52
   erigena 52
   herbacea (*E. carnea*) 51, 52-3
     'SPRINGWOOD WHITE' **53**
   terminalis 51
   tetralix 53
   vagans 53
Escallonia:
   bifida 53

   macrantha 53
   'SLIEVE DONARD' **53**
   varieties 53
Eucalyptus:
   caesia 54
   calophylla 54
   eximia 54
   ficifolia 54
   macrocarpa **54**, 54
   phoenicia 55
   pyriformis 55
   × *rhodantha* **54**, 55
   torquata 55
Eucryphia 55-6
   cordifolia 56
   glutinosa **55**, 56
   × *intermedia* 'ROSTREVOR' 56
   lucida 56
   milliganii 56
   × *nymanensis* 'NYMANSAY' **55**, 56
Euphorbia 56-7
   milii (*E. splendens milii*) **56**, 57
   fulgens **56**, 57
   leucocephala 57
   pulcherrima **56**, **57**, 57

False Acacia 120-1
fences 146
Filbert 43
Flowering Currant 119-20
Forsythia 57-8
   'ARNOLD DWARF' 58
   'ARNOLD GIANT' **57**, 58
   × *intermedia* 58
     'SPECTABILIS' **58**
   ovata 'TETRAGOLD' 58
   suspensa 58
   viridissima 58
Forsythia: White 10-11
Fremontia 58-9
Fremontodendron:
   californicum 58-9
     'CALIFORNIA GLORY' **58**, 59, **59**
     'PACIFIC SUNSET' 59
   mexicanum 59
French Lavender 87
Fuchsia 59-61
   fulgens 60
   'LADY THUMB' 60
   'LENA' 60-1, **60**
   magellanica **59**, 61
   'MRS POPPLE' **60**, 61
   'TOM THUMB' 61

Gardenia 61-2
   jasminoides (*G. angusta*) **61**, 62
   spathulifolia 62
   thunbergia **61**, 62
Garland Flower 47
Garrya elliptica 62, **62**
Gaultheria:
   cuneata 63, **63**
   procumbens 63
   shallon 63, **63**

Gean 114
Genista:
   aetnensis 64, **64**
   hispanica 64
   lydia 64, **65**
   tinctoria 64-5
Ghost Tree 48
glossary of terms 156
Golden Chain Tree 85-6
Gorse, Spanish 64
grafting 153
Grevillea:
   alpina 65
   biternata 65
   caleyi 65
   juniperina 65, **65**
   rosmarinifolia 65-6
     'SPLENDENS' **66**
   sericea 66
   sulphurea 66
ground preparation 148
Guelder Rose 136
Gum Tree 54-5

Halimium lasianthum 66, **66**
Hamamelis 66-7
   × *intermedia* 'JELENA' **67**
   mollis 67, **67**
   vernalis 67
   virginiana 67
Handkerchief Tree 48
Harry Lauder's Walking Stick 42
Hazel 42-3
   Winter 41-2
Heath 51-3
Heather 26-7
Hebe 67-9
   albicans 69, **69**
   armstrongii 69
   'AUTUMN GLORY' **68**, 69
   'CARL TESCHNER' 69
   'JAMES STIRLING' 69
   macrantha 69
   'MIDSUMMER BEAUTY' 69, **69**
   'MRS WINDER' 69
   pinguifolia 'PAGEI' 69
   salicifolia **68**, 69
   'SIMON DELAUX' 69
   'SPENCER'S SEEDLING' 69
hedges 146
Hedysarum:
   coronarium 70, **70**
   multijugum 69-70
Helianthemum 70-1, **71**
   nummularium **70**, 71
     'WISLEY PRIMROSE' **70**
Helichrysum 102, **103**
herbaceous borders 146
Hibiscus 71-2
   rosa-sinensis **71**, 72, **72**
   syriacus 72
     'BLUEBIRD' **72**
     'RED HEART' **72**
Hillock Bush 100
Himalayan Honeysuckle 89

Hoheria 72-3
   glabrata 73
   lyallii 73, **73**
   sexstylosa 73
Holly-leaved Sweetspire 79
Hollyhock: Tree 71-2
Holodiscus discolor 73, **73**
Honey Myrtle 100
Honeysuckle 91-4
   Himalayan 89
Horse Chestnut 13-15
Hortensia 74
Hydrangea 74-6
   arborescens 75
     'ANNABELLE' 75
     'GRANDIFLORA' **74**, 75
   aspera 75
   heteromalla 76
   involucrata 76
     'HORTENSIS' **75**, 76
   macrophylla **74**, **75**, 76
     'BLUE WAVE' **74**, 76
   paniculata 76
   petiolaris 76
   quercifolia 76
   sargentiana **76**, 76
   serrata 76
Hypericum 76-8
   calycinum 77
   coris 77
     'HIDCOTE' **77**, 77
   inodorum 77
   × *moseranum* 78
     'TRICOLOR' **78**, 78
   olympicum (*H. polyphyllum*) **77**, 78
     'CITRINUS' 78
     'ROWALLANE' 78

Indian Chestnut 14
Indigo Bush 78-9
Indigofera 78-9
   heterantha **78**, 79
   potaninii 79
Itea:
   ilicifolia 79, **79**
   virginica 79

Jacaranda 79-80
Jacaranda mimosifolia (*J. ovalifolium*) 79, 80
Japanese Honeysuckle 93
Japanese Snowball 136
Japanese Snowbell 131-2
Japonica 32-3
Jasmine 80-1
Jasminum 80-1
   beesianum 81
   humile **80**, 81
   mesnyi (*J. primulinum*) 81
   nudiflorum 81, **81**
   officinale 81, **81**
   parkeri 81
   polyanthum **80**, 81
Jerusalem Sage 108
June Berry 15-16

Kalmia:
  angustifolia 82
  latifolia 82, **82**
  polifolia 82
Kangaroo Thorn 13
Kerosene Bush 104
Kerria:
  japonica **82**, 83
    'PLENIFLORA' 83, **83**
    'VARIEGATA' (*K. j.* 'PICTA')
    83
Killarney Strawberry Tree 18
Kolkwitzia amabilis 83-4, **83**

+ *Laburnocytisus adamii* 84-5, **84**
Laburnum 85-6
  alpinum **85**, 86
  anagyroides 86
  × *watereri* 86
    'VOSSII' **85**, 86
Laburnum, Pink 84-5
Laburnum, Scotch 86
Lacecaps 74, 75-6
Lantern Tree 44
Laurel:
  Mountain 82
  Sheep 82
Laurustinus 136
Lavandula 86-7
  angustifolia (*L. officinale*, *L. spica*, *L. spicata*) **86**, 87
    'HIDCOTE' 87
    'MUNSTEAD' 87
  stoechas **86**, 87
Lavatera:
  arborea 87-8
  olbia 88
    'ROSEA' **87**, 88
Lavender 86-7
layering 153, **153**
Leptospermum 88-9
  cunninghamii (*L. lanigerum*) **88**, 89
  humifusum 89
  scoparium 89
    'RED DAMASK' 88
Leycesteria:
  crocothyrsos 89
  formosa 89, **89**
Ligustrum:
  japonicum 'ROTUNDIFOLIUM' 90
  lucidum 90, **90**
  ovatifolium 90
  quihoui 91
  sinense 91
  × *vicaryi* 91
  vulgare **90**, 91
Lilac 132-3
  Californian 30-1
Ling 26-7
Liriodendron:
  chinensis 91
  tulipifera 91, **91**
Lonicera 91-4
  × *americana* 92

× *brownii* 92-3
caprifolium 93
fragrantissima 93
× *heckrottii* 93
henryi 93
involucrata 93
japonica 93
  'AUREO-RETICULATA' 93
  'HALLIANA' 93
nitida 91-2
periclymenum **93**, 93
  'BELGICA' **93**, 93
  'SEROTINA' 93
pileata 93-4
× *tellmanniana* **92**, 94
tragophylla **92**, 94

Madrona 18
Magnolia 94-7
  campbellii 95
  denudata (*M. heptapeta*) 96
  grandiflora 94, **94**, 96
    'EXMOUTH' 96
    'FERRUGINEA' 96
    'GOLIATH' 96
  × *highdownensis* 96, **96**
  kobus 94, 96, 97
  macrophylla 96
  quinquepeta (*M. liliiflora*) 96
  sieboldii 96
  sinensis 97
  × *soulangiana* **96**, 97
  stellata **95**, 97
  wilsonii 97
Mahonia:
  aquifolium 97-8
  bealei 98
    'BUCKLAND' 98
    'CHARITY' 98
  japonica **97**, 98
    'LIONEL FORTESCUE' 98
  lomariifolia 98
  × *media* 98
    'UNDULATUM' 98
    'WINTER SUN' 98
Mallee 55
Mallow, Tree 87-8
Malus 98-100
  baccata 99
    'ELEYI' 99
  floribunda **98**, 99
  hupehensis 99
    'LADY NORTHCLIFFE' **99**, 99
    'LEMOINEI' 99
    'PROFUSION' **98**, 99
    'ROYALTY' 100
  tschonoskii 100
Manuka 88-9
Marri 54
Mediterranean Heath 52
Melaleuca:
  decussata 100
  fulgens 100
  hypericifolia 100, **100**
  incana 100
  lateritia 100

steedmanii 100
Mexican Orange 33-4
Mezereon 47-8, **47**
Mimosa 12-13
mixed borders 146
Mock Orange 106-8
Mount Etna Broom 64
Mountain Laurel 82
Mountain Rose 112
Moutan 105
Myrtle:
  Bog 82
  Scarlet Honey 100
  Totem Pole Honey 100

Nerium oleander 101, **101**

Ocean Spray 73
Oleander 101
Olearia 101-2
  × *haastii* 102, **102**
  macrodonta 102
  × *mollis* 102
  nummularifolia 102
  phlogopappa (*O. stellulata*) 102
  × *scilloniensis* 102
  semidentata 102, **102**
Orange, Mexican 33-4
Orange Peel Clematis 38
Oregon Grape 97-8
Ornamental Cherry 113-15
Ornamental Quince 32-3
Osmanthus 102-3
  × *burkwoodii* 103, **103**
  decorus 103
  delavayi 103, **103**
  fragrans 103
  heterophyllus (*O. ilicifolius*) 103
  × *Osmarea burkwoodii* 103
Ozothamnus:
  ledifolius 103-4
  rosmarinifolius 103-4, **104**

Pacific Dogwood 41
Paeonia 104-5
  delavayi 105, **105**
  × *lemoinei* 105
  lutea 105
    'LUDLOWII' **104**, 105
  suffruticosa 105, **105**
    'ROCK'S VARIETY' 105, **105**
Peach Protea 112
Pear-fruited Mallee 55
Peony, tree 104-5
pergolas 147
Periwinkle 137
Perovskia atriplicifolia 106, **106**
pests 154
Philadelphus 106-8
  'BEAUCLERC' **106**, 107
  'BELLE ETOILE' 107, **107**
  'BURFORDENSIS' 107
  'BURKWOODII' 107
  c. 'VARIEGATUS' 107
  coronarius 'AUREUS' 107
  'ENCHANTMENT' 107

'MANTEAU D'HERMINE' 107
microphyllus 107
  'SILVER SHOWERS' 107
  'SYBILLE' 108, **108**
  'VIRGINAL' **107**, 108
Phlomis:
  fruticosa 108, **108**
  italica 108
  purpurea 108
Pieris:
  'FIRECREST' 109
  'FOREST FLAME' 109
  formosa forrestii 109
  f.f. 'WAKEHURST' 109, **109**
  japonica 110
    'BLUSH' 110
  taiwanensis 110
Pineapple Broom 46
Pink Laburnum 84-5
planting 148-9
Plumbago, Shrubby 31-2
Poinsettia 57
Poppy, Tree 121
Potentilla 110-11
  'ABBOTSWOOD' **110**
  arbuscula 111
  cultivars 111
  davurica 111
    mandeburica 111
    'ELIZABETH' **110**
  fruticosa 111
  parvifolia 111, **111**
  × *sulphurascens* 111
Primrose Jasmine 81
Privet 90-1
propagation 151-3
Protea 111-12
  amplexicaulis 112
  caffra 112
  cynaroides 112, **112**
  grandiceps **111**, 112
  longifolia 112
  magnifica 112, **112**
  nana 112
  scolymocephala 112
pruning 149-50, **150**
Prunus 113-15
  'ACCOLADE' 113
  'AMANOGAWA' **113**, 114
  avium 114
  × *blireiana* 114
  cerasifera 114
  × *cistena* 114
  dulcis 114
  glandulosa 114
  'KANZAN' 114, **115**
  'KIKU-SHIDARE SAKURA' **114**, 114
  padus 114
  'PANDORA' 114
  sargentii 114
  serrulata 114-15
  'SHIROFUGEN' 115
  'SHIROTAE' 115, **115**
  subhirtella 'AUTUMNALIS' 115
  'TAI HAKU' 114

tenella 115
  'FIRE HILL' **114**
triloba 115
  'UKON' **113**, 115
  × *yedoensis* 115

Quince, Ornamental 32-3

Ragwort 128-9
Red Buckeye 15
Red-flowering Gum 54
Rhododendron 115-19
  arboreum **116**, 117, **118**
  augustinii 117
  'AVALANCHE' **113**
  campylocarpum 117-18
  cinnabarinum 118
  ferrugineum 118
  hybrids 118-19
  keiskei 118
  luteum **116**, 118
  maximum 118
  ponticum 118
  thompsonii 118, **119**
  wardii 118
  williamsianum 118
  yakushimanum 118, **118**
Rhus cotinus 43
Ribes:
  americanum 119
  × *gordonianum* 119
  laurifolium 119, **120**
  odoratum 119
  sanguineum 119-20
  speciosum 120
Robin Redbreast 100
Robinia:
  hispida 120, **120**
  kelseyi 120
  p. udacacia 121, **121**
Rock Rose 34-6, 70-1
Romneya:
  coulteri 121, **121**
  × *hybrida* 121
  trichocalyx 121
Rosa 122-5
  'CANARY BIRD' **123**
  'DOROTHY PERKINS' **124**
  'ENA HARKNESS' **122**
  'FANTIN-LATOUR' **123**
  'FRAGRANT CLOUD' **122**
  'FRAU DAGMAR HARTOPP'
    124
  'ICEBERG' **125**
  'KIFTSGATE' **123**
  'PINK PARFAIT' **122**
  'ZEPHIRINE DROUHIN' **125**
Rose 122-5
  climbers 123, 125
  floribundas 122, 125
  hybrid teas 122, 125

ramblers 123, 125
shrub 122-3, 124-5
species 124
Rose, Alpine 118
Rose, Mountain 112
Rose, Rock 34-6
Rose, Sun 70-1
Rose Mallee 55
Rose of Sharon 71-2, 77
Rosemary 125-6
  Bog 16
Rosmarinus 125-6
  officinalis 126, **126**
Rouen Lilac 133
Rubus 126-7
  odoratus 127
  spectabilis 127
  × *tridel* 126, 127
Russian Sage 106

Sage:
  Jerusalem 108
  Russian 106
St John's Wort 76-8
Salmonberry 127
Santolina:
  chamaecyparissus 127, **127**
  pinnata 127
  rosmarinifolia 127
Sarcococca 127-8
  hookeriana 'DIGYNA' **128**
Sargent Cherry 114
Scarlet Gum 55
Scarlet Honey Myrtle 100
Scarlet Plume 57
Scotch Heather 26-7
Scotch Laburnum 86
screens 146
seed sowing 151
Senecio 128-9
  bicolor cineraria 129
  compactus 129
  greyi **129**, 129
  laxifolius **128**, 129
  reinoldii 129
  'SUNSHINE' 129
Sheep Laurel 82
shrubberies 146
Shrubby Plumbago 31-2
Shrubby Ragwort 128-9
Shrubby Veronica 67-9
site preparation 148
siting trees and shrubs 145-7
Smoke Bush 43-4
Snowball, Japanese 136
Snowy Mespilus 15-16
soil 147
Solanum 129-30
  crispum 130
  'GLASNEVIN' **129**, 130
  jasminoides 'ALBUM' **130**, 130

Spanish Broom 130
Spanish Gorse 64
Spartium junceum 130, **130**
specimen plants 147
Spike Winterhazel 42
Spirea 130-1
  'ARGUTA' ('BRIDAL WREATH')
    131, **131**
  japonica (*S. bumalda*) 131
  nipponica 131
  thunbergii 131
  × *vanhouttei* 131
Spurge 56-7
staking 149, **149**
Strawberry Tree 17-18
Styrax:
  americana 132
  hemsleyana 132
  japonica 131, 132, **132**
  obassia 132
Sumach, Venetian 43-4
Sun Rose 70-1
Sweet Olive 103
Sweetspire 79
Sydney Golden Wattle 13
Syringa:
  × *chinensis* 133
  'SAUGEANA' 133
  × *hyacinthiflora* 133
  × *josiflexa* 'BELLICENT' 133,
  meyeri 'PALIBIN' 133
  microphylla **132**, 133
  × *persica* 133, **133**
  reflexa 133
  vulgaris 132, **132**, 133

Tamarisk 134
Tamarix:
  parviflora 134
  ramosissima (*T. pentandra*) 134,
    134
  tetrandra 134
Tassel Bush 62
Tea Tree 88-9
Totem Pole Honey Myrtle 100
Tree Heath 52
Tree Hollyhock 71-2
Tree Hydrangea 75
Tree Mallow 87-8
Tree Peony 104-5
Tree Poppy 121
trellises 147
Tricuspidaria dependens 44
Tulip Tree 91

Venetian Sumach 43-4
Veronica, Shrubby 67-9
Viburnum 134-6
  'ANNA RUSSELL' 135
  betulifolium 135
  × *bodnantense* 135, **135**

× *burkwoodii* 135, **136**
× *carlcephalum* 135
carlesii 135, 136
cinnamomifolium 135
davidii 135-6
farreri (*V. fragrans*) 136
× *juddii* 136
lantana 136
× *opulus* 136, **136**
plicatum 136
rhytidophyllum 136
sargentii 136
tinus 135, **135**, 136
tomentosum 136
  'PLICATUM' **134**
Vinca:
  difformis 137
  major 137, **137**
  minor 137, **137**
Viola cornuta 110
Virginia Sweetspire 79

walls 146
Wattle 12-13
Weeping Bottle Brush 26
Weigela:
  'ABEL CARRIERE' 138
  'BRISTOL RUBY' 138, **139**, 139
  'CANDIDA' 139
  'EVE RATHKE' 139
  florida 139
    'VARIEGATA' 138, **138**, 139
  middendorffiana 139, **139**
  'NEWPORT RED' 139
  'PRAECOX VARIEGATA' 139
White Forsythia 10-11
White Lace Bush 57
Winter Hazel 41-2
Winter Jasmine 81
Winter Sweet 33
Wintergreen, Creeping 63
Wisteria 139-41
  floribunda 140
    'ISSAI' **141**
    'MULTIJUGA' **140**
  sinensis **139**, 140, 141
Witch Hazel 66-7
Woolly Tea Tree 89

Yellow Bloodwood 54
Yucca 141-3
  filamentosa 142
  flaccida 143
  gloriosa 143
    'NOBILIS' **143**
    'VARIEGATA' **143**
  recurvifolia 143
  whipplei 141, 143

Zenobia pulverulenta 143, **143**

Photo Credits

Gillian Beckett, page 22; Bill Mason, page 144.